Online pornography

Online Pornography

Other Books of Related Interest:

Opposing Viewpoints Series

The Internet

Technology and Society

At Issue Series

Policing the Internet

Does the Internet Increase the Risk of Crime?

Current Controversies

Censorship

"Congress shall make
no law . . . abridging
the freedom of speech,
or of the press."

First Amendment to the U.S. Constitution

The basic foundation of our democracy is the First Amendment guarantee of freedom of expression. The Opposing Viewpoints series is dedicated to the concept of this basic freedom and the idea that it is more important to practice it than to enshrine it.

OPPOSING VIEWPOINTS® SERIES

Online Pornography

Emma Carlson Berne, Book Editor

GREENHAVEN PRESS

An imprint of Thomson Gale, a part of The Thomson Corporation

THOMSON

——★——™

GALE

Detroit • New York • San Francisco • New Haven, Conn. • Waterville, Maine • London

8/07

86109896

Christine Nasso, *Publisher*
Elizabeth Des Chenes, *Managing Editor*

© 2007 Thomson Gale, a part of The Thomson Corporation.

Thomson and Star logo are trademarks and Gale and Greenhaven Press are registered trademarks used herein under license.

For more information, contact:
Greenhaven Press
27500 Drake Rd.
Farmington Hills, MI 48331-3535
Or you can visit our Internet site at http://www.gale.com

LIBRARY OF CONGRESS CATALOGING-IN-PUBLICATION DATA

Online pornography / Emma Carlson Berne, book editor.
   p. cm. -- (Opposing viewpoints)
  Includes bibliographical references and index.
  ISBN-13: 978-0-7377-3657-1 (hardcover)
  ISBN-13: 978-0-7377-3658-8 (pbk.)
  1. Internet pornography. 2. Intellectual freedom. 3. Censorship. 4. Internet--Law and legislation. 5. Children and pornography. 6. Internet and children. I. Berne, Emma Carlson.
  HQ471.O55 2007
  363.4'702854678--dc22

                                   2007010677

ISBN-10: 0-7377-3657-7 (hardcover)
ISBN-10: 0-7377-3658-5 (pbk.)

Printed in the United States of America
10 9 8 7 6 5 4 3 2 1

Contents

Chapter 3: Should Children Be Protected from Online Pornography?

Chapter 4: Should Limits Be Placed on Online Pornography?

Why Consider Opposing Viewpoints?

"The only way in which a human being can make some approach to knowing the whole of a subject is by hearing what can be said about it by persons of every variety of opinion and studying all modes in which it can be looked at by every character of mind. No wise man ever acquired his wisdom in any mode but this."

John Stuart Mill

In our media-intensive culture it is not difficult to find differing opinions. Thousands of newspapers and magazines and dozens of radio and television talk shows resound with differing points of view. The difficulty lies in deciding which opinion to agree with and which "experts" seem the most credible. The more inundated we become with differing opinions and claims, the more essential it is to hone critical reading and thinking skills to evaluate these ideas. Opposing Viewpoints books address this problem directly by presenting stimulating debates that can be used to enhance and teach these skills. The varied opinions contained in each book examine many different aspects of a single issue. While examining these conveniently edited opposing views, readers can develop critical thinking skills such as the ability to compare and contrast authors' credibility, facts, argumentation styles, use of persuasive techniques, and other stylistic tools. In short, the Opposing Viewpoints series is an ideal way to attain the higher-level thinking and reading skills so essential in a culture of diverse and contradictory opinions.

In addition to providing a tool for critical thinking, Opposing Viewpoints books challenge readers to question their own strongly held opinions and assumptions. Most people form their opinions on the basis of upbringing, peer pressure, and personal, cultural, or professional bias. By reading carefully balanced opposing views, readers must directly confront new ideas as well as the opinions of those with whom they disagree. This is not to simplistically argue that everyone who reads opposing views will—or should—change his or her opinion. Instead, the series enhances readers' understanding of their own views by encouraging confrontation with opposing ideas. Careful examination of others' views can lead to the readers' understanding of the logical inconsistencies in their own opinions, perspective on why they hold an opinion, and the consideration of the possibility that their opinion requires further evaluation.

Evaluating Other Opinions

To ensure that this type of examination occurs, Opposing Viewpoints books present all types of opinions. Prominent spokespeople on different sides of each issue as well as well-known professionals from many disciplines challenge the reader. An additional goal of the series is to provide a forum for other, less-known, or even unpopular viewpoints. The opinion of an ordinary person who has had to make the decision to cut off life support from a terminally ill relative, for example, may be just as valuable and provide just as much insight as a medical ethicist's professional opinion. The editors have two additional purposes in including these less-known views. One, the editors encourage readers to respect others' opinions—even when not enhanced by professional credibility. It is only by reading or listening to and objectively evaluating others' ideas that one can determine whether they are worthy of consideration. Two, the inclusion of such viewpoints encourages the important critical thinking skill of objectively evaluating an author's credentials and bias. This evaluation will illuminate an author's reasons for taking a particular stance on an issue and will aid in readers' evaluation of the author's ideas.

It is our hope that these books will give readers a deeper understanding of the issues debated and an appreciation of the complexity of even seemingly simple issues when good and honest people disagree. This awareness is particularly important in a democratic society such as ours in which people enter into public debate to determine the common good. Those with whom one disagrees should not be regarded as enemies but rather as people whose views deserve careful examination and may shed light on one's own.

Thomas Jefferson once said that "difference of opinion leads to inquiry, and inquiry to truth." Jefferson, a broadly educated man, argued that "if a nation expects to be ignorant and free . . . it expects what never was and never will be." As individuals and as a nation, it is imperative that we consider the opinions of others and examine them with skill and discernment. The Opposing Viewpoints series is intended to help readers achieve this goal.

David L. Bender and Bruno Leone,
Founders

Introduction

"Internet pornography has become so popular partly because it offers a level of anonymity never available before."

—BBC

American society has always been concerned about morality, including deviant sexual behavior. Despite this concern, pornography has been present in various forms since the earliest days of the country. As media have changed, pornography has changed along with them, from printed material such as leaflets, postcards, booklets, and magazines, to films, television, videos, and, finally, to the digital domain and pornography's newest frontier: the Internet.

While pornography has always incited reprimands and anxiety from the community at large, the advent of the Internet and the enormous success of pornography in this new medium have ignited an entirely new firestorm of controversy. Part of the concern stems from the immense popularity of online pornography. The National Research Council estimated that by 2007, Internet pornography would become a seven-billion-dollar-a-year business. Not surprisingly, the vast majority of online pornography users are men: According to comScore, a company which measures Internet traffic, sixty-six percent of men between eighteen and thirty-four who use the Internet look at online pornography at least once a month.

Alarm over online pornography is not a new debate. In 1995, *Time* magazine ran a cover featuring the headline "On a Screen Near You: Cyberporn." Inside the issue, then-senator Dan Coats of Indiana called online pornography "a unique, disturbing and urgent circumstance." The magazine reported, "The press is on alert, parents and teachers are up in arms and lawmakers in Washington are rushing to ban the smut from cyberspace with new legislation." Over a decade later the concern has not abated. In 2005, CBS called online pornography "the biggest business on the web and a driving force behind a growing epidemic of sex addiction."

In large part, online pornography has sparked such worry because of the Internet's key difference from other media: the Internet has allowed pornography to move from a public arena to a private one. In previous eras, if people wanted to view pornographic material, they would have to engage in at least some sort of public behavior. They would have to go to a shop to purchase printed material, or meet a contact somewhere in order to obtain pornographic postcards or pictures. Theaters showing pornographic films, while often on the outskirts of towns or in other fringe areas, usually marked their presence with huge flashing signs advertising "XXX." Before the Internet, even videos, which could be viewed in the privacy of the home, had to be rented at an adult-video shop.

Online pornography, in contrast, can be located, obtained, and viewed *entirely* from the private space of the home. The user need not interact by phone, mail, or face-to-face with another person at all. In addition, the supply of pornography is virtually endless, if a user has a credit card.

This move from generally public spaces to private ones has raised issues about pornography with which society had never before grappled. Previously, people depended on a sort of public "eye" to keep viewers of pornography in check. Many rightly assumed that being forced to ask someone, face-to-face, for material or buying a ticket at a theater would feel shameful to the pornography user. This overarching societal disapproval was often enough to keep users from obtaining pornography too often or from obtaining even more deviant forms, such as child pornography or violent pornography. The community "eye" still serves as a powerful influence that very often encourages others to regulate their own potentially deviant behavior.

Online, however, the community eye loses its power. A user never has to expose his behavior to others by venturing into public spaces. He or she can remain almost entirely anonymous when obtaining pornography. Professor Elizabeth Englander told news station WKYC in Cleveland, Ohio, that "all kinds of deviant behavior pops up a little bit more on the [Internet] because people feel as though what they do online doesn't count. . . . Anything that makes people feel anonymous makes them more likely to act impulsively or to act on things that are deviant or [that] they otherwise wouldn't do." Antipornography activists argue that, protected by this veil of privacy, those who may have otherwise restrained themselves may feel freer to purchase child pornography, for instance. Philip Elmer-Dewitt of *Time* writes, "[With online pornography], you can only download those things that turn you on, rather than buy an entire magazine or video. You can explore different aspects of your sexuality without exposing yourself to communicable diseases or public ridicule."

While this concern about the loss of self-regulation is primary, the rise of Internet pornography also taps into a deeper societal concern: that technology has caused people to become more disconnected. As more and more interactions take place through a computer screen, people have become more private, many fear. They know less about their neighbors, for instance, and are less involved in the lives of those around them. For better or worse, pornography is also included in this concern.

There is little doubt that the issue of pornography on the Internet is far from resolved. Online porn is a hugely profitable business for thousands and a popular activity for millions. Through legislation, the courts, and the media, American society is grappling with aspects of pornography such as regulation, censorship, freedom of speech, and protection of children. The four chapters of *Opposing Viewpoints: Online Pornography* will present both sides of the debate in the following chapters: Is Online Pornography Harmful to Society? Is Online Pornography a Form of Free Speech? Should Children Be Protected from Online Pornography? Should Limits Be Placed on Online Pornography? This anthology will help clarify and illuminate these key issues.

CHAPTER 1

Is Online Pornography Harmful to Society?

Chapter Preface

A central issue surrounding the debate on online pornography—or indeed, any pornography—is that of the essential nature of pornographic material. American society has deemed pornography legal when it depicts and is marketed to adults. However, like many things that are legal but not necessarily healthy (tobacco, alcohol, television, just to name a few), the balance is an uneasy one. Some in society feel that, legal or not, looking at pornography is immoral, dangerous behavior that could start a user on a slippery slope to committing deviant sexual acts. Others feel that looking at adult pornography online is a harmless, pleasurable pastime—like watching television or eating junk food.

Those who consider online pornography dangerous and immoral tend to be socially conservative and concerned about morality in other areas of society also, such as in schools, libraries, or in other forms of media. The groups that have protested against the morality of online pornography have included right-wing political lobbying groups, such as the Concerned Women for America, and children's protection organizations, such as the Parents Television Council, which works to eliminate what it calls "smut" from all forms of media. These groups feel that to keep society safe, we must *protect* the vulnerable above all; pornography is seen as a danger, like a lit stove or a sharp knife. For instance, the antipornography group Morality in Media states,

> The production and distribution of hard-core pornography is a harmful . . . industry. . . . Hard-core pornography in the marketplace and indecency in the entertainment media are in many cases at least partly the cause of family breakup, unwed pregnancy, sexual violence, sexually transmitted diseases and other societal problems.

In contrast, groups that view online pornography as a harmless pastime tend to align themselves with concepts of free exchange of information and free speech. These groups include liberal and libertarian political groups such as the Cato Institute and the Free Speech Coalition, as well as those who work for Internet rights as a whole. For these individuals, the primary concern is individual freedom. As long as a pornography viewer is not breaking any laws, he or she should not be restricted or harassed. In fact, some of these groups argue, far greater harm lies in restricting pornography than in the actual pornography itself. The Adult Freedom Foundation (AFF), a pornography-rights group, states, "While adamantly against child pornography, AFF believes adults should be allowed to enjoy erotic entertainment and that the average adult accepts that right for other adults to choose lawful erotic entertainment."

This chapter will examine the relationship between morality and pornography from both sides of the debate.

> *"The easy access to . . . online porn is speeding up the dependence and escalation to harder-core material and more."*

Online Pornography Is Harmful

Jan LaRue

Jan LaRue is the chief counsel for the conservative lobbying group Concerned Women for America. In the following viewpoint, LaRue argues that the availability of online pornography materials leads to pedophilia and sex crimes with children. People don't just look at pornography on the Internet featuring pictures of consenting adults. Many users seek out Web sites with pictures of children and teenagers, LaRue writes. They make dates to meet these children in person and commit sex crimes with them. The presence of pornography on the Internet serves only to encourage these perverse desires, she argues.

As you read, consider the following questions:

1. What is one myth about pedophiles and online pornography that LaRue names?

Jan LaRue, "The Road to Perversion Is Paved with Pornography," Concerned Women for America, May 2, 2006. www.cwfa.org. Reproduced by permission.

2. How many complaints of obscene material sent to a child did the National Center for Missing and Exploited Children receive between September and April 2006, according to the author?

3. How many hits will a "teen porn" search of the Web reveal, as reported by LaRue?

Millions of men and boys are falling for the destructive myth that looking at "adult" porn is normal, healthy and harmless for "regular guys." Way too many are finding themselves handcuffed between two cops, under arrest for sexual conduct with a kid. The hook-ups with kids are occurring on the main streets of U.S. cities and the dark alleys of the virtual world.

Experts estimate that 50,000 sexual predators prowl the Internet for children every day. As long as myth trumps truth, the next estimate could be 10 times what it is today. Stopping predators before they ravage our kids and grandkids will be insurmountable.

The easy access to millions of pages of online porn is speeding up the dependence and escalation to harder-core material and more.

The centerfolds no longer gratify? There's an unending supply of harder-core images instantly available within a few mouse clicks and free for the taking. Want deviant? There's deviant beyond anything uncorrupted minds can fathom. Want some younger "stuff"? There's "pseudo" child porn where young-looking adults dress and act like teens and even toddlers sucking a pacifier and hugging stuffed animals. Want real child porn when the pretend doesn't do it anymore? It's traded for free by perverts in Internet chat rooms and encrypted Web sites, and for sale, and raking in billions. Want kids? There's a virtual playground full of kids ready to chat, instant message, and eager to send digital photos and videos to other "kids." Want a pimp for a hook-up with a kid? No need to risk being seen picking up a kid in a red light district. Their pimps and slave masters are online.

"Men fly in, are met by pimps, have sex with a 14-year-old for lunch, and get home in time for dinner with the family," said Sanford Jones, the chief juvenile judge of Fulton County, Georgia.

Stop and read it again until you get it. Men are flying home to dinner with the wife and kids after having sex with a kid. Who *does* that?

Myths about Online Pornography and Pedophilia

Most people can't even handle thinking about it, so they mix more myth and some truth to relieve their discomfort:

- They're all pedophiles.

- All child molesters are pedophiles.

- There are more pedophiles than I realized.

- Pedophiles probably get married and have kids to hide who they are.

- Pedophiles are only into kiddie porn.

- Regular guys stick with adult porn.

- No guy I know would have sex with a kid.

- I'm no guy who would have sex with a kid.

Not every guy who has sex with a minor is a pedophile. Most aren't. You may need to read that again too.

There is a difference between pedophiles who prefer to have sex with children and child molesters who prefer to have sex with adults but will have sex with a child if the situation presents itself. And it presents itself big time on the Internet.

For the child, it couldn't matter less what the clinical definition of his or her molester may be. What should matter to the rest of us is stopping "regular guys" from becoming child molesters.

Sex Crimes Are Rampant

According to [journalists Verna] Gates and [Mickey] Goodman [who wrote the article "Sex Tourism Thriving in U.S. Bible Belt," printed by Reuters on April 6, 2006]:

"Half of the street-level prostitutes in Atlanta are believed to be under 18, according to experts. Others are booked through Internet sex sites and from social sites like Black Planet, where girls innocently post profiles. . . . In March, police arrested a Canadian man meeting a 14-year-old girl he found through the Internet. . . . Another man drove from North Georgia, with a bag containing a teddy bear, a love note and condoms, snorting methamphetamine on the way. He expected a 13-year-old girl, but instead found Heather Lackey, a corporal with the Peachtree City Police Department. . . . During the 1996 Olympics in Atlanta, one man kept boys and hosted sex parties nightly."

[In December 2006] a congressional committee heard the gut-wrenching testimony of a 19-year-old telling how he began operating his own commercial Web site where men could view sexually explicit photos he took of himself. Justin Berry's nightmarish story is that of a 13-year-old boy in a broken home allowed unsupervised access to a Webcam and the Internet. A lonely boy looking for friends and love in all the wrong places immediately "found" adult males who seduced him with attention, gifts and money. Personal meetings led to his sexual abuse, which led to him sexually exploiting other boys by encouraging them to join the sordid business.

The National Center for Missing & Exploited Children's latest weekly report indicates that its *Cybertipline* has received "2,589 complaints of unsolicited obscene material sent to a child" from September 1, 2002, through April 9, 2006. Worse yet are the "15,995 complaints of online enticement of children for sexual acts" in the last [several] years. . . .

Men and boys: Beware before you click the mouse one more time and take a step closer to becoming one of the bad guys. . . .

Seeking Out Teen Porn

"Karen," who didn't want her real name used, was married for 11 years to her second husband before she discovered shocking images on his computer. "Usually girls, but sometimes boys, who are just over 18, but who are marketable because they look like they're under 18," said Karen. Her emotions went from confusion and anger to fear for her teenage daughter after discovering the collection. "I was very concerned that he was going to begin to sexualize her and her friends," said Karen.

"Karen's" husband became a threat to his own child after starting down a dark, dead-end road with no safety rails, no warning signs and no speed limit. The "adult" porn industry paves the road, operates the toll gates, and cares nothing about who's wrecked and ruined along the way.

Ask yourself:

1. What kind of "adult" markets a product that portrays "kids" as sex objects?

2. Who is the porn industry pandering to by producing and distributing "teen porn"?

3. Who believes that what we feed our minds doesn't affect our behavior?

A "teen porn" search of the World Wide Web on any given day will provide 7 to 8 million "hits." And "regular guys" like Karen's husband are hitting on it. . . .

Does "teen porn" "titillate"? A Web search on April 15, 2006, combining the term "soliciting minor for sex" with"pornography," produced 256,000 "hits."

Definition of a Pedophile

In a manual on child sexual abuse, the U.S. Department of Health and Human Services defines a pedophile as "an adult whose primary sexual interest is in children."

David Greenfield, psychologist and author of the book *Virtual Addiction*, says the Internet creates a sense of disinhibition. "People do and say things online that they never would do otherwise. The people I see in my office—they're not perverts, but they get online and suddenly, they're sex fiends."

Kenneth Lanning, a former FBI profiler, believes many offenders have harbored and suppressed deviant urges for years. "They may never have acted out. They were able to control it, and along comes the Internet . . . which is like pouring fuel on smoldering embers."

A word to "regular guys": "Can a man scoop fire into his lap without his clothes being burned?"

Sex Acts with Children

[In April 2006] a 26-year-old "with a fear of flying" flew from Massachusetts to Alabama after allegedly paying $1,200 for three hours of videotaping "two or three 10- to 12-year-old girls performing oral sex on him." His e-mail "order" says that "pigtails, freckles, and school uniforms would be a plus." FBI agents took Luke Simon Goljan, an "independent film producer for ITV Direct of Beverly Hills" into custody.

Michael William Schleicher, a high school band teacher, was arraigned in Anoka County, Minnesota, district court March 24, 2006, and charged with two counts of first-degree criminal sexual conduct and one count of soliciting a minor for sex. Schleicher allegedly solicited teenage girls for sex and used his live-streaming video Web cam to practice and record sex acts. "In his home, several computers and disks containing child and adult pornography were discovered," according to the complaint.

The office of the U.S. Attorney for the Southern District of New York announced the arrest of Timothy McDarrah on September 14, 2005, on charges of using the Internet to entice someone he believed to be a 13-year-old girl to engage in sexual activities. According to the complaint, McDarrah allegedly responded to an advertisement in the "erotic services" section of the popular Internet Web site "craigslist," offering the "freshest, youngest girls" available in all ages, and specified in graphic terms the sexual activity he desired.

An individual expecting sex with a 12-year-old had with him a duffle bag containing a digital camera, tripod, a video camera, four sections of nylon rope, one bottle of "Secret Passion love lotion [sic]" and a short story titled "The Seduction of an Angel." The story detailed an incestuous relationship between a father and his 16-year-old daughter. After the National Center for Missing & Exploited Children received a cybertipline report on April 8, 2003, federal and state law enforcement took the suspect into custody when he arrived at a Knoxville, Tennessee, hotel.

Pornography Is Dangerous and Degrading

A judge in a child pornography case opined that "if it were necessary for literary or artistic value, a person over the statutory age who perhaps looked younger could be utilized" in a sex scene.

Other than perverts and pornographers, who thinks the judge had in mind an entire genre of porn marketed as "teen," "young," "little," "virgin," "fresh," "ripe," "tender," or "cheerleader," or that it has any "literary or artistic value"?...

Whether one of you "regular guys" ends up running over a child, your drive down the dead-end porn road is hurting you and those you care about. Every mile defiles your thoughts about women and girls and affects the way you treat your mother, sister, friend, co-worker, wife, daughter and the rest of us. You can't consume degrading depictions and descriptions of women and "teens" and continue to treat us with respect as human beings.

Stop now and call for help if you need it. Otherwise, be prepared for the day when you need a mouse to reach the only "women" willing to spend time with you.

> *"In some situations, erotic material can be a healthy outlet for sexual fantasy."*

Online Pornography Can Be Harmless

Liza Featherstone

In the following viewpoint, author Liza Featherstone argues that while viewing online pornography can be a problem for some people, it can also be a positive, healthy experience. Couching her discussion in terms of established couples, Featherstone points out that couples can look at pornography on the Internet together as a way to add passion to their sex life. Featherstone acknowledges that for online pornography to be a positive experience, both members must be in agreement about the reason for viewing pornography. Liza Featherstone is a freelance journalist who frequently writes for the Nation *magazine.*

As you read, consider the following questions:

1. According to the author, why do some women feel betrayed by pornography?

2. What is one positive effect pornography can have on couples, according to David Schnarch, a psychologist cited by Featherstone?

Liza Featherstone, "You, Me, and Porn Make Three," *Psychology Today*, vol. 38, October 2005, pp. 82–87. Copyright of *Psychology Today,* property of Sussex Publishers, Inc. Reproduced by permission.

3. What might be one negative reason that some women or men turn to pornography in a marriage, according to the author?

When her new boyfriend confessed that he looked at porn, Donna, 37, made her views clear to him. "I'm very anti-pornography," she says. "I think it's very degrading to women, I told him. This is something I can't have in a relationship." He assured her that he'd only been interested in porn because he was single and lonely. Then, [in 2004], after the two had been married nine months, she found out he'd never stopped, at times spending as much as $120 a month on Internet raunch.

Donna, who lives in a small town in Connecticut, was stunned. "I blamed myself—I wasn't attractive enough. I have a weight problem—I blamed it on that." She also worried that she was overreacting: "Was I too strict? Too moral? Missing something?" Beyond her doubts about herself, she had a larger problem to deal with: "It broke my trust in the marriage."

Porn-gazing—whether chronic or casual—can become an explosive issue for a couple, corroding intimacy and demolishing the sexual connection. But reactions to pornography can be as varied as human desire itself, and fault is often in the eye of the beholder. For couples who already have sexual conflicts or difficulty trusting each other, porn can play a particularly destructive role. Yet in some situations, erotic material can be a healthy outlet for sexual fantasy, possibly bringing a couple closer together. Even a conflict over pornography, handled constructively, can improve a relationship.

Erotic images are more available—and more mainstream—than ever. According to comScore, which measures Internet traffic, 66 percent of Internet-using men between the ages of 18 and 34 look at online porn at least once a month. In the past, guys hid their liking for smut; now, they can openly embrace it, thanks to [porn star] Jenna Jameson, *Stuff* magazine and a porn-friendly culture. As a result, pornography-related conflicts among couples are becoming more common, marriage counselors say. The argument often has a similar refrain: He looks at it, she hates it and each resents the other. In a 2003 study published in the *Journal of Sex and Marital Therapy*, Ana Bridges and her co-authors found that while most women weren't bothered by their partner's X-rated interest, a significant minority were extremely distressed by it. But are they right to be worried? Is the anguish misdirected—or is there something to fear about porn?

Unrealistic Expectations

Many women feel betrayed by porn, even though their mates don't necessarily perceive it as a transgression. "It was infidelity" says Suzanne Vail, 43, of Nashua, New Hampshire, describing her ex-boyfriend's habit. "I felt cheated on." More than a quarter of the women in Bridges's study agreed. The feelings may arise from an unrealistic understanding of fantasy in adult sexuality, suggests marital therapist Michele Weiner-Davis, author of *The Sex-Starved Marriage* and founder of Divorce-Busting, a therapy and coaching service aimed at saving marriages. Partners, even long-term ones, may have never discussed fantasies. "On the conservative end of the spectrum, some wives are upset that the husband would think about any other images or other women," she says. "I'm just amazed at that—some of these couples have been together a long time!"

Weiner-Davis will often try to "do a little sexual education," explaining that fantasy is normal and that a lot of people enjoy sexually explicit images—especially men, who tend to be more visually oriented. If that "doesn't make a dent, if the wife is truly beside herself, it is a betrayal and I treat it as such." Weiner-Davis doesn't necessarily agree that a husband in this situation is cheating, but the emotional dynamics are much the same: The porn user needs to understand his partner's hurt feelings, and she needs to find a way to forgive him.

Many women feel that the guy who looks at porn must harbor some hostility toward women. Yet research hasn't established a link between pornography consumption and misogyny. One 2004 study found that porn users actually had slightly more positive and egalitarian views of women than other men did, though porn users were also more likely to hold stereotypical beliefs—for example, that women are more moral.

It's a counterintuitive finding, likely to annoy both conservatives and antiporn feminists. But simultaneously liking porn and respecting women is consistent with a liberal outlook, which typically combines tolerance with an egalitarian perspective. If your boyfriend has an abortion-rights bumper sticker and a stash of hardcore smut on his computer, he may be Jerry Falwell's worst nightmare, but he's not all that unusual. Or perhaps the connection between porn watching and pro-female attitudes is more fundamental, suggests James Beggan, a University of Louisville sociologist who co-authored the study with psychologist colleagues at Texas Tech University. "If you spend your time looking at pictures of naked women" he observes, "that's not really consistent with not liking women. It's consistent with liking them."

Normal Worries

Phil, a 46-year-old writer in New York City, doesn't enjoy porn that much. But when it first became readily available online, the novelty sucked him in. "In the early days of the Internet, I would sometimes surf through reams of online flesh" he recalls wryly, "but I found it numbingly repetitive, and the opposite of arousing." Partly out of boredom, Phil (not his real name) used some of the images to teach himself graphic design. When his wife found the files on his computer, "she

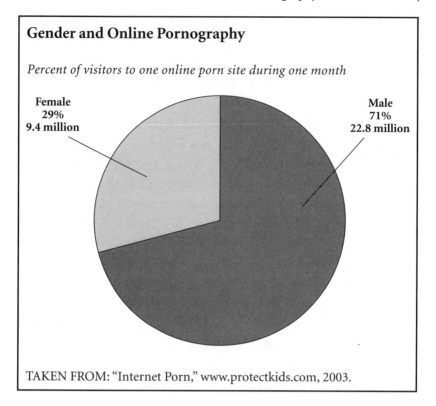

Gender and Online Pornography

Percent of visitors to one online porn site during one month

Female
29%
9.4 million

Male
71%
22.8 million

TAKEN FROM: "Internet Porn," www.protectkids.com, 2003.

freaked," he recalls. "I was just pasting women's heads on different naked bodies—you know, perfectly normal behavior," he jokes, "but it did not sit at all well with the real-life woman I was living with."

Phil's wife was the kind of gorgeous blonde that most men only fantasize about, yet he suspects that his looking at porn made her feel inadequate. He was bewildered. Any notion that he was looking at cheesy Internet images because she wasn't good enough, he says, "would have been wildly misguided." (The couple has since divorced for other reasons.)

That fear is very real for many women, who worry they can't compete with the airbrushed perfection of the porn star. And they are "absolutely right," says Barry McCarthy, author of *Rekindling Desire*, and a therapist in Washington—they can't. But not measuring up to an illusion shouldn't be cause for worry, he adds. What makes the woman in porn so erotic is not her red lips and her fake breasts, but the fact that she's "crazy" says McCarthy. She's ever ready, always willing to do anything to please a man. No real woman could or would want to be that way.

Psychologically healthy men don't have much trouble distinguishing between reality and the weird world of commercial raunch. The trouble emerges, McCarthy says, when a person "can't differentiate between fantasy and reality: 'Why isn't my girlfriend like that? Why isn't she into sex with animals? Why won't she let me ejaculate on her face?'" Suzanne Vail, who operates an online group for women who believe their partners are sex addicts, says women in her group have attempted to please porn-obsessed men through liposuction, breast surgery and crash dieting. If a man has a driving need to make his real-life partner into a porn star, he's got a problem. A woman who acquiesces in such an impossible pursuit may quickly find that she's got one, too.

Pornography Can Be Positive

Porn can actually help foster emotional and sexual intimacy, says Colorado psychologist David Schnarch, author of *Resurrecting Sex*, who runs a couples therapy practice with his wife. He explains: "A significant portion of our work in helping couples develop a deeper sexual connection is through erotic images. Erotica, as well as couples' own masturbatory fantasies, can be useful tools for helping them develop as adults." How couples intensify their sexual relationship differs radically depending on the individuals and on the dynamic between them. But fantasy is certainly a part of a healthy sex life, and porn does contribute significantly to the archive of sexy scenarios in our heads. It can also inspire couples to experiment more.

Interestingly, in Ana Bridges's study, the women with the most positive views of porn's role in their relationship were engaged in a more creative activity: The couples were taking sexy pictures of one another, removing entirely the problem of competition with the busty and lascivious commercial sex bomb. "It's very validating," says Bridges. "It's me turning you on. Even in my absence, you want to look at me."

While men do look at porn more than women do, the ease and privacy of the Internet allow many women who would never have dared in the past to explore this realm. Fully half of the women in Bridges's study said they looked at pornography themselves.

Problems with Sex Addiction

And women can become just as obsessed as men. Jennifer Schneider, an M.D. who has studied sex addicts, interviewed several women who became hooked on smut. One 35-year-old married woman said the pictures (especially those depicting S&M [sado-masochistic] scenarios) "would haunt me day and night." The habit began to erode her marriage. "My husband could no longer satisfy me," she told Schneider. "I wanted what I saw in the videos and pictures and was too embarrassed to ask him for it." The woman said she was freed from her obsessions by God, but a good marital therapist might have viewed this as an opportunity for the couple to learn to talk to each other about their desires—and perhaps try something new.

There is little solid research on how men feel about their female partner's porn use—or, for that matter, on how porn figures into gay relationships, which could help illuminate how much a straight couple's porn conflict is really a matter of gender differences. Some men clearly find it sexy, perhaps seeing her porn interest as a sign of a woman's experimental nature or aggressive libido. But writer Pamela Paul argues in her new book, *Pornified: How Pornography Is Transforming Our Lives, Our Relationships and Our Families*, that while many men hope their partner approves of (or at least tolerates) their own porn interest, they may be critical of a girlfriend or wife who uses pornography herself. A 2004 *Elle*-MSNBC.com poll found that six in ten men were concerned about their partner's interest in Internet smut.

Dose matters. According to research by the late Alvin Cooper of the Silicon Valley Psychotherapy Center, people engaged in any kind of online sexual activity for less than an hour a week said it had little impact on their lives; people using it for 11 or more hours a week said it affected both their self-image and their feelings about their partners. Anywhere between one and ten hours a week is ambiguous terrain. It may just be a way to release stress, but as Cooper has pointed out, "the Internet is . . . a very powerful force that people can quickly develop a problem with, like crack cocaine."

Donna's husband, Steve, was just such a person. "Before, the pain and embarrassment of buying a magazine or going into a sex shop would stop him," she says. "Once he got the computer, that was it." Some individuals are vulnerable to compulsive porn use because of their own psychological makeup. Steve is a diagnosed obsessive compulsive, and in his case, the availability and anonymity of Internet porn lent itself to ritualistic, uncontrollable behavior. But online pornography can become an obsession even for people without psychological disorders, simply because it is so easily available and taps into such a powerful appetite.

Complex Reasons for Viewing Porn

Not everyone is going to embrace porn as a positive force. But it is usually possible to work through the conflicts posed by pornography use. Michele Weiner-Davis encourages couples to explore what it means in the dynamic of the relationship: Why does it bother her so much? Is there something he gets from it that he could be getting from the relationship? "Sometimes it is relational," she says. "For example, the wife may not understand the importance of a good sex life. Sometimes she's not experimental or passionate. If, in a long-term marriage, couples don't have a common goal of keeping marriage passionate," she says, an X-rated habit can be a symptom of restlessness.

A heavy reliance on porn may be an outgrowth of other sexual discontents. Many men complain that their wives have gained weight and are no longer very attractive, says Weiner-Davis. Others prefer smut to real sex because while they're viewing porn, they're in control, McCarthy and Weiner-Davis agree. Says McCarthy, "Couple sex is much more complicated." Says Bridges, "People think it's just a way to masturbate, but in a relationship it can be a punishment: 'I don't want to be with you right now.'"

In the case of one couple Bridges saw, the husband had pulled away from his wife's constant criticism and retreated into fantasy. She had to learn not to be so mean, says Bridges. While there are countless ways to withdraw from a spouse, porn is both satisfying and readily available. And because it's sexual, it's a far more loaded distancing strategy than playing golf or spending too much time at the office.

One solution to the porn dilemma that clearly doesn't work: surveillance. It undermines trust and can foster its own obsessions. Suzanne Vail says partners may get compulsive about monitoring, just as those married to drug addicts or alcoholics can become overly involved in policing addictions.

Researchers and therapists concur that couples are better off treating the conflict as a practical matter rather than a moral issue. Faith may not be such an important consideration: Bridges found that nonreligious women were just as likely as religious women to be upset over a partner's porn use. "Looking at this in terms of right or wrong isn't helpful" says Weiner-Davis. "There's a great deal of variation in what turns people on, and the question is: What can we as a couple do about it?" As she points out, couples work hard to reach agreement on many issues—how they will spend money, where they will live, whether they will have children—but often neglect to achieve any sort of consensus on their sex life: how often, what sort of activities, how much extracurricular interest is acceptable.

A couple may never see eye-to-eye on porn; even if he's not compulsive, she may always feel that it's disgusting (or immoral). As David Schnarch has often pointed out, tolerating discomfort—and recognizing that a partner's desires may be different from yours—is critical to a fully adult, intimate sexual relationship. Then again, if porn is repellent to someone you love, it may be worthwhile to call it quits, like smoking or other cherished habits we give up for the sake of a relationship. As Weiner-Davis says of porn, "You won't get a disease, but it could cost you your marriage."

> *"Untold thousands of . . . children have become unknowing participants in the online pornography industry."*

Online Pornography Is a Growing Moral Problem

Kurt Eichenwald

Kurt Eichenwald is a reporter for the New York Times. *The following viewpoint is an excerpt of testimony Eichenwald provided for a Congressional hearing on Internet pornography. Eichenwald argues that rather than dismissing online pornography as some do, parents and citizens should take the issue very seriously. Online pornography is a highly sophisticated, organized business that almost anyone can access. It is not a safe place for adults to enjoy licit sexual images, Eichenwald writes, but rather a dangerous venue often involving children and adolescents who are tricked into performing pornographic acts on Webcams.*

As you read, consider the following questions:

1. According to the author, why are chat rooms no longer necessary for predators to find children online?

2. What is a portal and what use would one be to a predator online, according to Eichenwald?

Kurt Eichenwald, testimony before the Oversight and Investigations Subcommittee of the House Energy and Commerce Committee, April 4, 2006. http://energycommerce .house.gov/reparchives/108/Hearings/04042006hearing1820/Eichenwald.pdf.

3. What are two of the reasons the author gives why children might be lured into pornography online?

As a citizen, I was dumbfounded by what I found. As a father, I was terrified. Like most people I gave little thought during my life to the scourge of child pornography. But I now know that we are fighting a losing battle.

The predators are sophisticated in the use of computers and talented in their manipulation of children. They count on our willingness to avert our eyes from the unpleasant to succeed in their pursuit of illegal images of minors. And we have been far too willing to comply. That is part of why the child pornography business has exploded in the past decade. . . . [It']s now a $20 billion-a-year industry.

Webcam pornography has emerged in just the last few years but is already a significant part of this illicit industry. . . . Hundreds of minors have been lost to the lure of performing in online pornography. I interviewed a number of them. They include children from every walk of life, wealthy and middle-class, poor, honors students and those struggling with their grades, children of divorce and with intact families. The only shared characteristic I found is [that] a loneliness that these minors feel is alleviated by meeting people online and in person through their webcam business.

A Well-Constructed System

Entire infrastructures have emerged to sustain this business, including both witting and unwitting corporate participants. You have already heard how predators have turned the ingenuity of some of our greatest online companies against our children. Wish lists with companies like Amazon.com and American Eagle Outfitters—a wonderful convenience for gift-giving—have become mechanisms for seducing children. Online payment systems such as PayPal.com have been used to facilitate transfers of cash. Communications programs from

Cr8zysue13: A Case Study

People [magazine] set up accounts with AOL and Yahoo! under the name Cr8zysue13 and established a profile with her age (13), location (New York City) and favorite music (Nine Inch Nails and Marilyn Manson). We clicked a box saying we were 18. Then we went surfing. On Web browsers and in chat rooms, "Cr8zysue13" was barraged with sexuality in every form. In a "romance" chat room she was propositioned; she was deluged with racy junk e-mails and instant messages, many with links to sites where anything goes—bestiality, orgies and S&M. "Kids are going to see things they've never seen in their lives," says cyberporn expert Parry Aftab. "It's unbelievable stuff you wouldn't be able to buy in most porn stores. We need to prepare kids for this."

Richard Jerome,
People, *April 26, 2004.*

companies like AOL and Yahoo are used both for direct conversations between predators and children and for the transmission of illegal video images. We've heard a lot today about chatrooms. They're no longer necessary. A predator can reach each child individually through these communication systems. Many of these programs and services can be obtained by children in minutes without requiring accurate identification or proof of either age or parental consent.

But in addition to the unsuspecting companies, there are businesses that know exactly what they are doing. In my reporting, I discovered credit card processors who provided support for webcam child pornography. I found Web-hosting companies that offered servers for the illegal businesses. I even found a company that provided streaming video to sites operated by minors on condition that the company president be allowed to watch the pornographic performances for free.

I also located scores of marketing sites, known as portals, which were used to direct potential customers to the webcam child-pornography sites. These portals . . . underscore the scope and magnitude of this business. I have a listing maintained by a single portal of the almost 600 teenage webcam sites that it marketed. Perhaps most disturbing was that major American and international companies advertise on these marketing portals for child pornography. The advertisements . . . appeared immediately above images used by boys and girls to market their pornographic sites. Apparently, these companies were attempting to win business both from customers and the teenage pornographers themselves as they offered services to help efficiently run more pay-sites. . . .

No Sites Are Safe

But the for-pay sites of adolescents are only one level of this illicit business. Untold thousands of other children have become unknowing participants in the online pornography industry. These minors perform not for money or gifts but because they have been tricked into stripping and masturbating online for what they believe is a single viewer. These performances are recorded and then posted on for-pay pornography sites without the knowledge or consent of the minor. . . . I found websites dedicated to offering webcam videos of hundreds of girls and boys who had been duped into such performances. . . .

There is a business infrastructure for this part of the industry as well. There are people who make their living trolling the Internet for children with webcams, luring them into sexual performances and selling the resulting pornographic videos. To aid such people and others in disguising their true identities, there is software available that allows anyone to make a recorded video appear to be a live webcam transmission. The result is that a middle-aged man can portray himself as a teenage boy or girl complete with the video needed to convince any doubters.

I discovered a group of predators who took bets among themselves about how many online approaches it would require to convince a girl with a webcam to take off her clothes, with a resulting recorded video shared among the bettors. By the time I found this group, they had played their game dozens of times. They appear to have never failed to convince their target to strip. . . .

To aid in their hunts for adolescents, these adults again use legitimate businesses. . . . Numerous listings of children, including sites such as MySpace.com and BuddyPick.com are now the favored sites, the virtual Sears catalogue for pedophiles. Using these sites in combination, predators can search for children by age, location, and sex. They can obtain enormous amounts of identifying data, including whether a child operates a webcam. I have witnessed conversations among child predators online where they discuss the latest minor located from these sites. . . . Even social-networking sites that boast of being safe engage in reckless behavior, requiring personal data from minors before allowing access to their sites, reinforcing the children's false view that providing such information is harmless.

Easy to Find Children Online

When I explained how predators used these systems to the producers for Oprah Winfrey, they asked me for a demonstration. We limited my search to minors within twenty miles of my location, meaning, if I was a pedophile, I could personally meet those minors within the hour. The producers timed me. It took only a minute and thirty seconds before I was in direct contact with a sixteen-year-old girl. By that time I knew her name, address, school, plans for the evening and other identifying information, including her younger sisters' names and

ages. We repeated the test searching for a boy within the same distance. This time, they wanted to make it harder and asked me to make sure the kid had a webcam. I was in contact with a fourteen-year-old in two-and-a-half minutes. In both instances, I told these minors what I was doing and advised them not to speak with strangers online. Both replied, contrary to the obvious, that they never did. . . .

After my story [was published] a university professor e-mailed me and made postings about the Internet to complain that, statistically, few viewers of child pornography become molesters. As you have heard [from other, previous testimony], his statistics are bogus. But his argument, applied to this circumstance, is ludicrous. These are not instances where pedophiles are obtaining images of children they cannot identify. Here, a single child is being fed upon by hundreds of predators, all in direct, daily contact. The entreaties to meet begin quickly. Numerous minors told me of predators pleading for meetings. More than a few, I believe, agreed to go.

I have found oftentimes that adults react to these facts with incredulity. They cannot comprehend how a child could be so easily lured into pornography or speak so readily to a stranger. . . . But you also have to understand the environment where the minors find themselves. They are not being approached by some stranger in the park. Rather, they are in their own homes, feeling safe. They feel comfortable on the Internet, in ways we may not recognize. Internet communication has all of the elements of true social interaction but remains shallow. So it is both socially fulfilling and emotionally non-threatening. There is no one else there, just a small, silent device nearby. There is a level of unreality about it and on the part of the minors, a simple lack of comprehension. . . .

Each year, each week, each day the predators are becoming more sophisticated with computers, facilitating the growth and evolution of child pornography. It is why this business is exploding. . . . [We] are woefully behind.

> "*[The moralizers] will learn that Liberty itself is the most enduring and universal American moral value.*"

Online Pornography Is Not a Moral Problem

J.D. Obenberger

J.D. Obenberger is a lawyer who represents the adult entertainment industry in his practice. He has written extensively on the issue of pornography rights and access. In the following article, Obenberger argues that since a very large segment of American society enjoys pornography, especially online pornography, it cannot be classified as a moral problem. Instead, it is what Obenberger calls the "sermons" of those who oppose pornography that are the problem in society. Free access to pornography is a right of all Americans, Obenberger writes, and people are demanding it.

As you read, consider the following questions:

1. What fundamental right does the author feel is threatened by the political climate at the time of writing?

2. What definition does Obenberger provide for the word "prurient?"

3. Which online technique has complicated the issue of online pornography, according to the author?

The American people form the largest single market for explicit, sexually-oriented entertainment in the world. As I write these words, millions of Americans are accessing pay websites, choosing pay per view on their home cable connection, selecting in-room hotel movies, and renting adult DVD's and videotapes. In theory, someone could count all of this commerce and study the demographics, which seem to point to the conclusion that adult, erotic productions now experience such widespread acceptance that they can be called commonplace. Recreational erotica seems to cut across all strata of our society with a democratic disregard of race, creed, education, income, and generation. Beyond those trackable events, vast numbers of Americans are seeking free erotica on "thumbnail gallery posts" on the Internet, in the newsgroups, in peer-to-peer file sharing networks. Of course, untold numbers will be replaying DVD's and tapes they have already purchased and video clips they have previously downloaded. Americans have taken the availability of all of this for granted.

But, in the high corridors of power, there is a storm brewing against all of this. There are those who want to marshal all of the force, power, and might of the United States government against all of this, and put a permanent end to explicit adult entertainment. . . .

The American people sense that we live in times that are particularly scary for the survival of Liberty and Americans of every political stripe feel it. Some in the incumbent [George W. Bush] Administration feel that their 51% majority [in Congress as of the November 2004 elections] has given them a mandate to broadly apply a repressive moral agenda. . . .

The moralizers imagine the customers of the adult Internet to be a small number of thrill seekers and a larger number of pitifully addicted perverts. . . . Such an assessment of the

Definition of Liberty

Liberty consists in the freedom to do everything which injures no one else; hence the exercise of the natural rights of each man has no limits except those which assure to the other members of the society the enjoyment of the same rights. These limits can only be determined by law.

Declaration of the Rights of Man and of the Citizen, *1789.*

situation belies the numbers: More than fifty percent of pay per view in American hotels is hardcore. The cable TV services in every important American market provide hardcore erotica. It is rather a pitiful few troubled cranks who stand on the sidewalk to protest the erotic, expressive products of adult bookstores. The reality that some in power refuse to accept is that mainstream American moral values about candor in the depiction of sex have changed beyond their power to imagine.

Access to Pornography Is a Right

There are those of us who think that personal Liberty is a moral value, too. In fact, our ancestors chose to put the word *Liberty* on all American coins. They might have chosen "Decency" or "Moral Order" or "Law and Order" or even "United We Stand," but they chose *Liberty*. The immigrants arriving by ship in New York harbor did not look up to the Statue of Decency; They saw the Statue of Liberty, and if co-existing with some perceived indecency was the price of breathing their own free air, it was a choice they were generally delighted to elect because the price of freedom includes tolerance of the freedom of others.

Under existing American law, that which can be called criminally obscene must appeal to a "prurient" (shameful or morbid—diseased or loathsome) interest in sex, nudity, or excretion and be patently offensive in its depiction or description of those matters. Prurience and patent-offensiveness are each judged in the law according to contemporary community standards.

We know that the Adult Industry serves the demand of millions of Americans every day—and that these customers form the large majority of those Americans who do have strong feelings about what our society accepts or tolerates. They want the products which are offered. Sermons by the moralizers will never or rarely be offered on cable pay per view, nor will they ever amount to 50% of in-room movies. No one is very likely to sign up for a $29.95 per month (recurring) website with the offerings of the moralizers. There won't be much traffic in their sermons on peer-to-peer networks. I don't think we'll ever see the day of popular thumbnail gallery posts featuring what they have to offer. It doesn't seem likely that stores with their literature will remain profitably open twenty-four hours per day. "Community Standards," you see, encompasses materials which enormous numbers of Americans actually demand. Large numbers of Americans are willing to pay substantial sums for the offerings of the Adult Internet and few would pay much to hear the rants of the would-be censors. It is for that reason that the very large majority of the erotic fare available commercially in the American market is not obscene under our existing laws. On some level, the moralizers know that and fear it because it shakes their faulty belief systems. By persecuting the Adult Industry, they seek a validation of their own extreme and fringe dogmas in our courts. In time, they will learn that Liberty itself is the most enduring and universal American moral value.

Spam Is a Separate Issue

The issues have been clouded by the spammers who assault unwilling viewers by jamming into their eyeballs potentially offensive material that the viewers don't want to see. They indiscriminately shill their wares in ways that expose both children and unwilling adults to it. Some few have used Internet domain names that mislead people to porn while they seek innocent information that is light-years away from the erotic. In so doing, they have generated untold animosity against an industry with which most Americans would have no controversy. Spam is not the issue, though the enemies of erotic expression seem to confuse the issue. Strong laws are now in place to avert this harm. . . .

The moralizers cause a disturbance in the Force. While proclaiming "community standards," they [do] not merely ignore the reality of what Americans accept, they marginalize what is now commonplace and normal. They work to turn back time to a more intolerant era. They aspire to wrest the notion of "community standards" away from a measure of what the people actually accept and want—perverting "community standards" into a measure of what they think righteous and God-fearing Americans should see. It troubles them that others see it differently. They desperately hope that by limiting supply, they will change the standards of American Society, which they now view as wicked and immoral. Their trial strategy [during court cases] will be to confuse jurors about the difference between modesty and shame—and about the difference between what is fit for children and what is available for willing adults. They will claim to "protect the children" as they go after what adults can see.

Supply and Demand

Even should they fool some juries, that they will fail to change American tolerance and demand is inevitable: The American market's demand will be fulfilled, whether from an American industry or from sources elsewhere that are not affected by American obscenity laws. Though they believe that pornography is a bad thing for people—and causes people and families trouble—and "pollutes" our culture and communities—we think they are generally very wrong—their energies will not make one whit of difference in the behavior of Americans in the era of the global Internet. The would-be censors not only misunderstand the American people, they misunderstand what the Internet means to censorship.

The winds we now feel from the approaching storm portend a struggle broadly between tolerance and intolerance, between freedom and control, between Liberty and repression. The battle we will wage—and win—is not a narrow struggle about what is permissible in porn, but is rather about the range of the human soul to freely dream, express, and receive. And in this struggle, we defend not only the Adult Industry and its customers, but the Liberty of the American People to make their own decisions about what they view, read, and hear in private. As an advocate for clients involved in the Adult Industry, I know that as I defend them, it will be with both feet planted firmly in the traditions, constitution, laws, and history of a free people. Their narrow, fringe, dogmatic zealotry will be exposed for what it is. Come what may, we shall together assure that the people who came to these shores in the hope of freedom will remain free.

| *"The Internet is the crack cocaine of sexual addiction."*

Online Pornography Is Addictive

Rod Gustafson

Rod Gustafson is a film critic who writes a newspaper and Internet column called "Parent Previews." In the following viewpoint, he argues that though scientific research explicitly on addiction to porn is scanty, anecdotal evidence and social scientists' findings prove that pornography is indeed addictive. Gustafson supports his argument by presenting information from a Senate hearing on pornography addiction. The experts at the hearing agreed that pornography is detrimental to mental health and relationships. Online pornography is even more harmful. Parents must protect their children from these images, Gustafson writes, and learn how to discuss pornography in a calm, informed way.

As you read, consider the following questions:

1. According to the author, pornography has moved from being a "lewd form of entertainment" to what?

2. Name two results of prolonged exposure to pornography identified by Dr. James Weaver, as cited by Gustafson.

3. What is one way that parents can discourage their children from viewing online pornography, according to the author?

You've done everything you can. You filter your Internet connection. The V-chip is activated in your television. The parental lock is set on all your DVD players. And you keep an eye on video games and music coming through the door. But, even with all these precautions (which few families actually have put in place), there is still a reasonable chance your family will be affected by the influence of pornography.

We will examine some of the latest research regarding pornography, and what we know and suspect about its influence on our families. Most of the information presented will be based on a hearing titled "The Science Behind Pornography Addiction," presented to the Senate Subcommittee on Science, Technology, and Space on November 18, 2004.

To this point, there is little verified research available to confirm what the presenters at this hearing (and many of us) already suspect: That pornography has moved from being a lewd form of entertainment to a significant societal concern, which is breaking up families, destroying lives, and causing economic losses.

Regardless of the scanty scientific studies, the discussion led by [Senator] Sam Brownback (R-Kansas) certainly revealed the presenters—all PhDs who have researched this area extensively—have had personal and professional experiences to convince them pornography is having a negative impact on our nation.

Setting the tone of the meeting, Senator Brownback declared, "Over the last few decades, the nature of, and access to, sexually explicit material in the marketplace has been radically transformed and expanded. With the advent of the Internet and video technology, the problem of addiction to sexually explicit material has grown exponentially in size and scope."

Pornography Statistics

Here are a few of the numbers he gathered on the issue:

- 72 million users visit Internet pornography sites each year.

- One expert in cybersex addiction asserts that 15% of individuals visiting on-line porn sites develop sexual behavior that interferes with their lives. (Although he did not specifically name the expert, he attributed it to the same individual who coined the phrase, "The Internet is the crack cocaine of sexual addiction.")

- One in five children, ages 10 to 17, have received a sexual solicitation over the Internet.

- Nine out of ten children, ages 8 to 16 who have Internet access, have visited porn websites, usually in the course of looking up information for homework.

- According to the founder of the *Center for Online Addiction*, approximately 65% of people who visit their site, do so because of marital problems created by cyber pornography.

As an interesting side note, Sen. Brownback also shared this information:

"At a recent meeting of the American Academy of Matrimonial Lawyers, two-thirds of the divorce lawyers who attended said excessive interest in online pornography played a significant role in divorces in the past year."

Sen. Brownback quoted Richard Berry, President of the Academy, who said, "This is clearly related to the Internet. Pornography had an almost non-existent role in divorce just seven or eight years ago."

Like his colleagues [also presenting at the hearing], Dr. [James] Weaver recognized the lack of controlled scientific study in this area, explaining, "Unfortunately, research directly assessing the impact of pornography addiction on families and communities is limited."

However, he offered evidence from the broader area of social science research he and others have compiled. These are some of his comments regarding the results of prolonged exposure to pornography:

- Initial reactions of discomfort and disgust dissipate rapidly with repeated exposure and are replaced by unadulterated reactions of enjoyment.

- Prolonged use leads to many distorted perceptions, including the belief that promiscuous behavior is healthy, whereas sexual repression constitutes a health risk.

- Men create a sexual callousness toward women.

- Both women and men who use porn are more likely to trivialize rape and nonviolent forms of sexual abuse of children, as a criminal offense.

- It spawns doubts about the value of marriage as an essential social institution and about its future viability. It also diminishes the desire to have children. (The strongest effect of this kind concerns the aspiration of female viewers for female children.)

- It fosters sexual dissatisfaction among both men and women.

Dr. Mary Anne Layden, Co-director of the Sexual Trauma and Psychopathology Program at the University of Pennsylvania touched on economic losses from pornography.

"70% of the hits on Internet sex sites occur between 9 and 5 on business computers. Research also indicates, and my clinical experience supports, that 40% of sex addicts will lose their spouse, 58% will suffer severe financial losses, and 27% to 40% will lose their job or profession."

Questions About "Net Nannyism"

Is monitoring your kids' Internet activity—say, reviewing the Web sites they've visited—a violation of their rights or a paradigm of parental responsibility? At what age is this Net nannyism appropriate? When kids are just learning to surf the World Wide Web, certainly, but it's not as if you can stop worrying once the training wheels are off. One mother told me she discreetly checks the porn sites in her teenage son's history folder to make certain they're not too extreme. I cringed, too, but her approach may be realistic; teenage boys will be teenage boys, and they're not just looking at centerfolds these days.

Ruth Marcus,
Washington Post, *March 7, 2006.*

Warnings of Pornography's Danger

If there is any doubt about pornography's involvement with those who commit sex crimes, Dr. Judith Reisman of the California Protective Parents Association reminded the audience of a 1984 Senate Hearing at which John Rabun, now the head of the Department of Justice's Missing and Abducted Children Center, testified. He was involved in researching sex crimes, and said during his testimony, "all, that is 100% of rapists, pedophiles, etc., in their study, possessed adult pornography."

It's important to remember these are observations as opposed to properly controlled studies. Yet, with these preliminary results coming in, it appears the tip of the iceberg has just been spotted. For your family, this may be the early warning you need to avoid a collision with tragic results.

Putting Internet filtering in place (along with the other measures mentioned at the beginning of this article) is a must, but parents need to be prepared to discuss pornography with their children when it happens (as opposed to *if* it will happen).

Here are just a few tips that seem common to many who are offering advice in this area:

Keeping Children Away from Pornography

Prevention:

- Talk to your children about the statistics you have learned in this article. Help them to understand how pornography lies to them about healthy sexual relationships, and how these lies can cause emotional, physical, and even economic distress in their lives.

- Frequently encourage open and honest communication between you and your children on all sexual subjects (along with drugs and any other "difficult" topics). It's so much easier to address these issues prior to a "crisis" moment. Have a regular "date night" or time when you can privately discuss these issues one-on-one with your children.

- Keep any computers with Internet connections in the busiest areas of your home. This makes it difficult for users to "sneak a peek" at inappropriate material.

- Use some sort of Internet filtering. There are many options available. . . .

- Activate your television's V-Chip along with the parental controls on your DVD players and satellite receivers. But remember that all of this technology depends on volunteer rating systems, and you still need to keep a close eye on who is watching what.

If your child sees pornography . . .

- Don't panic! This will discourage them from ever speaking to you again in the future.

- Let your child do most of the talking. Have them describe what they saw. Encourage them to use clinical terms for anatomical parts and actions.

- Where did they see it? Were other people present who may also be bothered by the incident?

- Ask them how they felt. What bothers you may not be as repulsive to them. Let them tell you about their feelings and objections to the experience.

- Discuss ways to avoid a reoccurrence.

- Gently remind them why you are concerned about pornography, but remember . . . they likely already know that, or they wouldn't be talking with you.

- Follow up after a few days. Our imaginations often make images become worse. Be careful not to drag your child through the entire event again, but gently probe to find out if it's still bothering them. If it is, discuss it further. Be reassuring, and help your child to have the confidence to know they can deal with this.

> "[The] notions of 'sexual addiction' generally, including 'pornography addiction' as well as the recent concern with 'on-line sex addiction' are highly questionable to most scientists."

Online Pornography Is Not Addictive

Daniel Linz

Daniel Linz is a psychologist and researcher at the University of California at Santa Barbara who studies pornography and its effects on human behavior. In the following viewpoint, Linz refutes the testimony of several experts at a Senate hearing on the science behind pornography addiction. According to Linz, pornography addiction has not been recognized by the scientific community as a valid diagnosis. Many factors must be considered when labeling behavior an "addiction." Many people do not display all the needed factors, yet are still labeled pornography addicts. In addition, science has not yet shown that viewing pornography has lasting, negative effects on a person.

Daniel Linz, "Statement of Daniel Linz, Response to Testimony Before the United States Senate on the Science Behind Pornography Addiction," Free Speech Coalition, November 2004. Reproduced by permission of the author.

As you read, consider the following questions:

1. According to the author, what are the four findings that emerge from an examination of the literature on sex addiction?
2. How does Linz define "addiction?"
3. According to Dr. William Fisher, cited by the author, what happened to the rate of rape in the United States during a period of rapid growth of Internet pornography?

My research for the last 25 years has involved scientifically testing the social psychological assumptions made by the law and legal actors in the area of the First Amendment and freedom of speech. This work spans the topics of media violence, pornography and other sex-oriented entertainment. My work on pornography and its effects on human behavior has been relied on extensively by the National Academy of Sciences, a private nonprofit society of distinguished scholars engaged in scientific and engineering research and appears in their recent publication, "Youth, Pornography and the Internet."

It has come to my attention that The Senate Committee on Commerce, Science, and Transportation held a hearing on "The Science Behind Pornography Addiction" on November 18, 2004. My understanding is that the Committee has allowed a two-week response period. I would like to take this opportunity to respond to the testimony of the several witnesses who testified before the committee. It is my opinion that a one-sided view of the "science" behind the notion of pornography exposure as addictive has been presented to the Committee. I would like to take the opportunity to present what I feel is a more objective overview of the state of scientific research than that expressed by the witnesses who appeared before the Committee.

No Evidence Supporting Pornography Addiction

Dr. [Judith] Reisman makes the claim that: "Thanks to the latest advances in neuroscience, we now know that pornographic visual images imprint and alter the brain, triggering an instant, involuntary, but lasting, biochemical memory trail, arguably, subverting the First Amendment by overriding the cognitive speech process. This is true of so-called 'soft-core' and 'hard-core' pornography. And once new neurochemical pathways are established they are difficult or impossible to delete." Later she asserts: "These media erotic fantasies become deeply embedded . . . addicting many of those exposed."

It is indeed a psychological fact that many powerful messages and ideas leave strong memory traces. This is in no way unique to pornographic images. Dr. Reisman fails to distinguish the nature of strong memory traces resulting from other experiences from pornography in her work. She appears to believe that once the viewer is exposed to enough pornography he or she loses the capacity to reason or make intelligent judgments about the messages being conveyed in pornographic material and that other memory traces from equally or more profound experiences are overwhelmed by exposure and subsequent "addiction" to pornography. There is no scientifically credible evidence for her ideas.

In fact, the notions of "sexual addiction" generally, including "pornography addiction" as well as the recent concern with "on-line sex addiction" are highly questionable to most scientists. Four findings seem to emerge from an unbiased examination of the psychological literature on sex addiction: 1) So-called sexual addiction may be nothing more than learned behavior that can be unlearned; 2) labels such as "sex addict" may tell us more about society's prejudices and the therapist doing the labeling than the client; 3) most research on pornography use, for example, through venues such as the Internet, is methodologically flawed; and, 4) scientists who have undertaken scientifically rigorous studies of exposure to sex materials report that despite high levels of exposure to pornography in venues such as the Internet, few negative effects are observed.

"Sex Addict" Is a Misleading Label

An addiction is commonly described as an experience of powerlessness, an unmanageable drive, and a basic out-of-control behavior. "Sexual addiction" may be nothing more than a learned sexual behavior expressed in violation of prevailing societal norms and expectations. In our society today it appears to be in vogue to attribute numerous popular behaviors to biological and psychological origins. It is an explanation of convenience for something threatening and unpopular. . . .

"It seems misleading to characterize behaviors as 'addictions' on the basis that people say they do too much of them," says Sara Kiesler, PhD, a researcher at Carnegie Mellon University and co-author of one of the only controlled studies on Internet usage, published in the September 1998 *American Psychologist*. No research has yet established that there is a disorder of Internet sex addiction that is separable from problems such as loneliness or problem gambling, or that a passion for using the Internet is long-lasting.

Labels such as "sex addict" or "pornography addict" may tell us more about our society and gender roles than shed light an any new syndrome. According to the American Psychological Association: Those diagnosed as "sex addicts" are disproportionately men, leading some researchers to hypothesize that the process of socialization along traditional "masculinity ideology" with respect to sex results in men expressing their masculinity through excessive sexual behavior. Labeling someone a sex addict may also be more a function of the therapist's values than an objective clinical evaluation. . . .

Other researchers report that despite high levels of exposure to pornography few negative effects are observed. In a

Opinion of a Pornography Webmaster

The last bit of significant research that the government commissioned showed porn to be unrelated to crime—why are we allowing the government to ignore this fact? While that research is getting up there in age, and the pornography business has changed, as has its content, the [George W.] Bush administration has shown no desire to commission a new round of independent, scientifically-backed studies to take a new unbiased look at the issue, instead preferring to spend millions of taxpayer dollars and jeopardize the freedom of American citizens based on the opinions of religious fanatics.

Connor Young, www.ynot.com, February 19, 2004.

study in the May 1998 issue of *Professional Psychology: Research and Practice*, Alvin Cooper, PhD, who is training coordinator at Stanford University's counseling and psychological services center, found that about 82 percent of Internet users spent less than an hour doing so, "with very few negative repercussions."

Previous Inclinations to Violence

Dr. [Jeffrey] Satinover hypothesizes that: "Initial hesitations to enjoy the material are rapidly lost with repeated exposure and give way to unadulterated reactions of enjoyment." Dr. Satinover's remarks include claims that: "Prolonged exposure to pornography stimulates a preference for depictions of group sex, sadomasochistic practices, and sexual contact with animals," and "trivializes nonviolent forms of the sexual abuse of children." However, while claiming that: "Prolonged exposure to pornography trivializes rape as a criminal offense," he admits that: "Psychotic men are strongly affected, whereas men with minimal psychotic inclination are not."

This last point is critical. Indeed, there is an enormous amount of research concerning the effects of experimentally induced exposure to sexually explicit materials. What does this research say?

If we know anything about pornography exposure and antisocial behaviors such as violence against women we know two things: 1) for the average person the message of violence as pleasurable to the woman must be present for negative effects to occur; and 2) for other forms of pornography the effects are an interaction between personality characteristics and exposure.

For example, [researchers] Linz, Donnerstein and Penrod in a study reported in the *Journal of Personality and Social Psychology*, found that exposure to violent films depicting violence against women desensitized men who viewed them and rendered the men less sympathetic towards a victim of sexual assault they were later asked to evaluate for injuries. This same effect was not observed for nonviolent pornography.

Once we move from the laboratory to investigations involving men who report viewing pornography, the effects of sexually explicit materials are almost certainly a joint function of the personality characteristics of the individual who seeks out such materials and of exposure to such materials per se. . . .

Not Supported by Science

Dr. [Mary Anne] Layden puts forth the notion that: "For the viewer, pornography increases the likelihood of sexual addiction and they respond in ways similar to other addicts. Sexual addicts develop tolerance and will need more and harder kinds of pornographic material. They have escalating compulsive sexual behavior becoming more out of control and also experience withdrawal symptoms if they stop the use of the sexual material."

In fact, contrary to Dr. Layden's speculation, the psychological and psychiatric community does not recognize "sexual addiction" and the related notion of "pornography addiction" as a distinct psychological disorder. The descriptive terms "sexual addiction" and "pornography addiction" do not appear in the current *Diagnostic and Statistical Manual of Mental Disorders (DSM-IV)*. According to Richard Irons, M.D. and Jennifer P. Schneider, M.D., Ph.D., addiction professionals who encounter both compulsive and impulsive sexual acting-out behaviors in their patients have experienced too many conceptual and communication difficulties with mental health professionals and managed care organizations who utilize *DSM* terminology and diagnostic criteria. This difficulty in communication has fueled so much skepticism among psychiatrists and other mental health professionals regarding the case for including sex addiction as a mental disorder that they have not recognized such a classification.

Dr. James Weaver correctly notes that: "Unfortunately, research directly assessing pornography addiction on families and communities is limited." The lack of scientific research on pornography addiction does not prevent Dr. Weaver from speculating that in this age of "cybersex" compulsive and/or obsessive use of pornography could have social repercussions. In other words, Dr. Weaver actually has no data on pornography addiction from his studies. In fact, his data do not speak to the notion of addiction at all, but rather to what he alleges are changes in attitudes and beliefs following forced exposure to pornography by college students. . . .

Finally, there is a real-life observation that is difficult to dispute. As an admittedly crude estimate of consequences of exposure to sexually explicit Internet materials on individuals who seek contact with such content, Dr. William Fisher in an article in the *Journal of Sex Research* made an informative observation. He plotted rates of reported forcible rape in the United States from 1995 to 1999. This time interval is by all accounts a period of exponential growth in the availability and use of all forms of Internet sexually explicit materials. Although open to a variety of interpretations, he noted that the rate of reported forcible rape in the U.S. fell consistently and significantly throughout this time period of spectacular increase in access to and use of Internet sexually explicit materials of all kinds.

Many Factors Considered

In summary, before rushing to the judgment that pornography is addicting, we must take note of the following: So-called sexual addiction may be nothing more than learned behavior that can be unlearned; labels such as "sex addict" may tell us more about society's prejudices and the therapist doing the labeling than the client; scientists who have undertaken scientifically rigorous studies of exposure to sex materials report that despite high levels of exposure to pornography in venues such as the Internet, few negative effects are observed. For the average person the message of violence against women must be present for negative effects to occur. For other forms of pornography the effects are an interaction between personality and exposure to pornography. Professionals who encounter both compulsive and impulsive sexual acting-out behaviors in their patients have experienced too many conceptual problems with the notion of sex addiction to be able to separate their preconceived ideas from whatever pathology they may observe in their patients. This difficulty in communication has fueled so much skepticism among psychiatrists and other mental health professionals regarding the case for including sex addiction as a mental disorder that they have not recognized such a classification.

Periodical Bibliography

The following articles have been selected to supplement the diverse view presented in this chapter.

David Amsden	"Not Tonight, Honey," *New York*, October 20, 2003.
Celeste Biever	"The Irresistible Rise of Cybersex," *New Scientist*, June 17, 2006.
Allison Fass	"Sex and the City," *Forbes*, February 17, 2003.
Katori Hall	"'My Husband's Addicted to Porn,'" *Essence*, June 2006.
Ben Hammersley	"Love Bytes: Porn.com," *Observer* (London), October 27, 2002.
Julie Hanus	"The Culture of Pornography Is Shaping Our Lives, for Better and for Worse," *Utne Reader*, September/October 2006.
Dirk Johnson	"Preachers and Porn," *Newsweek*, April 12, 2004.
Carol Lowes	"Overcoming Inertia on Porn," *Christianity Today*, September 2003.
Michele Mandel	"The Crack Cocaine of Porn: Cybersex," *Toronto Sun*, January 16, 2005.
Pamela Paul	"The Porn Factor," *Time*, January 19, 2004.
Richard Reeves	"Does Sex Make Us Happy? Don't Talk About It," *New Statesman*, March 28, 2005.
Amy Sohn	"A Laptop Never Says No," *New York*, May 30, 2005.
Adrian Turpin	"Not Tonight, Darling, I'm Online," *Financial Times* (London), April 1, 2006.
Naomi Wolf	"The Porn Myth," *New York*, October 20, 2003.

Is Online Pornography a Form of Free Speech?

Chapter Preface

The issue of the application of the First Amendment to Internet pornography is an important aspect of the debate. Through the courts, Americans have long upheld protection of pornography under free-speech laws, albeit a tenuous, frequently challenged protection. The invention of online pornography, however, has revived the debate anew. Those who believe that online pornography should indeed fall under First Amendment protection usually declare that the issue is one of censorship—illegal in the United States, where citizens are guaranteed a right to information. These groups tend to include general free-speech activists as well as purveyors of Internet porn.

Groups on the opposing side usually argue that the First Amendment protects speech, not images, and does not necessarily extend to the Web. Pornography, therefore, should be restricted without free-speech protection. Conservative, family-values-promoting organizations fall into this category.

In 1998, Congress entered the debate with the passage of the Children's Online Protection Act, or COPA. The law ordered all distributors of "obscene" material to restrict their sites from access by minors. However, the definition of "obscene" provided by the law was broad and could include potentially educational material such as art or health information. The law was challenged by the American Civil Liberties Union, and in 2004, the Supreme Court struck it down as unconstitutional on the grounds that it restricted free speech.

The decision, however, was not entirely clear. In the Court's opinion, Justice Clarence Thomas reminded the public that although "the First Amendment means that the government has no power to restrict expression because of its message, its ideas, its subject matter or its content," obscene speech is not necessarily protected under the First Amendment. But, he wrote,

> this Court struggled in the past to define obscenity in a manner that did not impose an impermissible burden on protected speech. . . . The difficulty resulted from the belief that "in the area of freedom of speech and press the courts must always remain sensitive to any infringement on genuinely serious literary, artistic, political, or scientific expression."

The balance between permitting free speech, avoiding censorship, and restricting obscenity is a delicate one. The viewpoints in the following chapter will represent an array of opinions on the issue.

> "Content-based prohibitions, enforced by severe criminal penalties, have the constant potential to be a repressive force in the lives and thoughts of a free people."

Online Pornography Should Be Protected as Free Speech

Anthony Kennedy

In the following viewpoint, the Supreme Court of the United States argues that some pornography on the Internet should be protected by the First Amendment. The Court upholds a lower court's decision to prohibit the enforcement of the Child Online Protection Act, or COPA. This act, writes Justice Anthony Kennedy, is too broad and places too many restrictions on free speech. Some speech, including forms of pornography, may indeed be regulated, Kennedy writes, but in the case of COPA, the law is both overly restrictive and ineffective. Filtering and blocking software has been shown to be more effective in protecting children from pornography on the Internet.

As you read, consider the following questions:

1. According to the author, what is the danger of content-based prohibitions?

Anthony Kennedy, opinion of the court, *Ashcroft v. ACLU*, 542 U.S., no. 03-218, Supreme Court of the United States, June 29, 2004.

2. What was the name of the 1996 act Congress passed before COPA, as cited by Kennedy?

3. Name two reasons why the Court prefers the use of filtering software over COPA, according to the author.

This case presents a challenge to a statute enacted by Congress to protect minors from exposure to sexually explicit materials on the Internet, the Child Online Protection Act (COPA). We must decide whether the Court of Appeals was correct to affirm a ruling by the District Court that enforcement of COPA should be enjoined [prohibited] because the statute likely violates the First Amendment.

In enacting COPA, Congress gave consideration to our earlier decisions on this subject. The imperative of according respect to the Congress, however, does not permit us to depart from well-established First Amendment principles. Instead, we must hold the Government to its constitutional burden of proof.

Content-based prohibitions, enforced by severe criminal penalties, have the constant potential to be a repressive force in the lives and thoughts of a free people. To guard against that threat the Constitution demands that content-based restrictions on speech be presumed invalid, and that the Government bear the burden of showing their constitutionality. This is true even when Congress twice has attempted to find a constitutional means to restrict, and punish, the speech in question. . . .

Laws to Protect Minors

COPA is the second attempt by Congress to make the Internet safe for minors by criminalizing certain Internet speech. The first attempt was the Communications Decency Act [CDA] of 1996. The Court held the CDA unconstitutional because it was not narrowly tailored to serve a compelling governmental interest and because less restrictive alternatives were available.

In response to the Court's decision [regarding the CDA], Congress passed COPA. COPA imposes criminal penalties of a $50,000 fine and six months in prison for the knowing posting, for "commercial purposes," of World Wide Web content that is "harmful to minors."...

Since the passage of COPA, Congress has enacted additional laws regulating the Internet in an attempt to protect minors. For example, it has enacted a prohibition on misleading Internet domain names, in order to prevent Web site owners from disguising pornographic Web sites in a way likely to cause uninterested persons to visit them. It has also passed a statute creating a "Dot Kids" second-level Internet domain, the content of which is restricted to that which is fit for minors under the age of 13.

Injunction Against COPA

Respondents [defendants in the case], Internet content providers, and others concerned with protecting the freedom of speech, filed suit in the United States District Court for the Eastern District of Pennsylvania. They sought a preliminary injunction [an order prohibiting action] against enforcement of the statute. After considering testimony from witnesses presented by both respondents and the Government, the District Court issued an order granting the preliminary injunction. The court first noted that the statute would place a burden on some protected speech. The court then concluded that respondents were likely to prevail on their argument that there were less restrictive alternatives to the statute: "On the record to date, it is not apparent ... that [petitioner] [in this case, the government] can meet its burden to prove that COPA is the least restrictive means available to achieve the goal of restricting the access of minors" to harmful material. In particular, it noted that "[t]he record before the Court reveals that blocking or filtering technology may be at least as successful as COPA would be in restricting minors' access to harmful material online without imposing the burden on constitutionally protected speech that COPA imposes on adult users or Web site operators."

The Government appealed the District Court's decision to the United States Court of Appeals for the Third Circuit. The Court of Appeals affirmed the preliminary injunction. . . . The Court of Appeals concluded that the statute was not narrowly tailored to serve a compelling Government interest, was overbroad, and was not the least restrictive means available for the Government to serve the interest of preventing minors from using the Internet to gain access to materials that are harmful to them. . . .

Restrict Speech Carefully

The District Court, in deciding to grant the preliminary injunction, concentrated primarily on the argument that there are plausible, less restrictive alternatives to COPA. A statute that "effectively suppresses a large amount of speech that adults have a constitutional right to receive and to address to one another . . . is unacceptable if less restrictive alternatives would be at least as effective in achieving the legitimate purpose that the statute was enacted to serve." When plaintiffs challenge a content-based speech restriction, the burden is on the Government to prove that the proposed alternatives will not be as effective as the challenged statute.

In considering this question, a court assumes that certain protected speech may be regulated, and then asks what is the least restrictive alternative that can be used to achieve that goal. The purpose of the test is not to consider whether the challenged restriction has some effect in achieving Congress' goal, regardless of the restriction it imposes. The purpose of the test is to ensure that speech is restricted no further than necessary to achieve the goal, for it is important to assure that legitimate speech is not chilled or punished. For that reason, the test does not begin with the status quo of existing regula-

The Dissenting Opinion

The Child Online Protection Act (Act), seeks to protect children from exposure to commercial pornography placed on the Internet. It does so by requiring commercial providers to place pornographic material behind Internet "screens" readily accessible to adults who produce age verification. The Court recognizes that we should "'proceed . . . with care before invalidating the Act,'" while pointing out that the "imperative of according respect to the Congress . . . does not permit us to depart from well-established First Amendment principles." I agree with these generalities. Like the Court, I would subject the Act to "the most exacting scrutiny," requiring the Government to show that any restriction of nonobscene expression is "narrowly drawn" to further a "compelling interest" and that the restriction amounts to the "least restrictive means" available to further that interest.

Nonetheless, my examination of (1) the burdens the Act imposes on protected expression, (2) the Act's ability to further a compelling interest, and (3) the proposed "less restrictive alternatives" convinces me that the Court is wrong. I cannot accept its conclusion that Congress could have accomplished its statutory objective—protecting children from commercial pornography on the Internet—in other, less restrictive ways.

Stephen Breyer, dissenting opinion, Ashcroft v. ACLU,
June 29, 2004.

tions, then ask whether the challenged restriction has some additional ability to achieve Congress' legitimate interest. Any restriction on speech could be justified under that analysis. Instead, the court should ask whether the challenged regulation is the least restrictive means among available, effective alternatives. . . .

As the Government bears the burden of proof on the ultimate question of COPA's constitutionality, respondents must be deemed likely to prevail unless the Government has shown that respondents' proposed less restrictive alternatives are less effective than COPA. Applying that analysis, the District Court concluded that respondents were likely to prevail.

Filters Less Restrictive than COPA

The primary alternative considered by the District Court was blocking and filtering software. Blocking and filtering software is an alternative that is less restrictive than COPA, and, in addition, likely more effective as a means of restricting children's access to materials harmful to them.

Filters are less restrictive than COPA. They impose selective restrictions on speech at the receiving end, not universal restrictions at the source. Under a filtering regime, adults without children may gain access to speech they have a right to see without having to identify themselves or provide their credit card information. Even adults with children may obtain access to the same speech on the same terms simply by turning off the filter on their home computers. Above all, promoting the use of filters does not condemn as criminal any category of speech, and so the potential chilling effect is eliminated, or at least much diminished. All of these things are true, moreover, regardless of how broadly or narrowly the definitions in COPA are construed.

Filters also may well be more effective than COPA. First, a filter can prevent minors from seeing all pornography, not just pornography posted to the Web from America. The District Court noted in its fact findings that one witness estimated that 40% of harmful-to-minors content comes from overseas. COPA does not prevent minors from having access to those foreign harmful materials. That alone makes it possible that filtering software might be more effective in serving Congress' goals. Effectiveness is likely to diminish even further if COPA is upheld, because the providers of the materials that would be covered by the statute simply can move their operations overseas. It is not an answer to say that COPA reaches some amount of materials that are harmful to minors; the question is whether it would reach more of them than less restrictive alternatives. In addition, the District Court found that verification systems may be subject to evasion and circumvention, for example by minors who have their own credit cards. Finally, filters also may be more effective because they can be applied to all forms of Internet communication, including e-mail, not just communications available via the World Wide Web.

Confirmed by Congress

That filtering software may well be more effective than COPA is confirmed by the findings of the Commission on Child Online Protection, a commission created by Congress in COPA itself. Congress directed the Commission to evaluate the relative merits of different means of restricting minors' ability to gain access to harmful materials on the Internet. It unambiguously found that filters are more effective than age-verification requirements. Thus, not only has the Government failed to carry its burden of showing the District Court that the proposed alternative is less effective, but also a Government Commission appointed to consider the question has concluded just the opposite.

Filtering software, of course, is not a perfect solution to the problem of children gaining access to harmful-to-minors materials. It may block some materials that are not harmful to minors and fail to catch some that are. Whatever the deficiencies of filters, however, the Government failed to introduce specific evidence proving that existing technologies are less effective than the restrictions in COPA. . . .

Incentives for Filtering

One argument to the contrary is worth mentioning—the argument that filtering software is not an available alternative because Congress may not require it to be used. That argument carries little weight, because Congress undoubtedly may act to encourage the use of filters. We have held that Congress can give strong incentives to schools and libraries to use them. It could also take steps to promote their development by industry, and their use by parents. It is incorrect, for that reason, to say that filters are part of the current regulatory status quo. The need for parental cooperation does not automatically disqualify a proposed less restrictive alternative. In enacting COPA, Congress said its goal was to prevent the "widespread availability of the Internet" from providing "opportunities for minors to access materials through the World Wide Web in a manner that can frustrate parental supervision or control." COPA presumes that parents lack the ability, not the will, to monitor what their children see. By enacting programs to promote use of filtering software, Congress could give parents that ability without subjecting protected speech to severe penalties. . . .

There are also important practical reasons to let the injunction stand pending a full trial on the merits. First, the potential harms from reversing the injunction outweigh those of leaving it in place by mistake. . . .

Second, there are substantial factual disputes remaining in the case. As mentioned above, there is a serious gap in the evidence as to the effectiveness of filtering software. . . .

Options for Congress

On a final point, it is important to note that this opinion does not hold that Congress is incapable of enacting any regulation of the Internet designed to prevent minors from gaining access to harmful materials. The parties, because of the conclusion of the Court of Appeals that the statute's definitions rendered it unconstitutional, did not devote their attention to the question whether further evidence might be introduced on the relative restrictiveness and effectiveness of alternatives to the statute. On remand [when a case is sent back to a lower court], however, the parties will be able to introduce further evidence on this point. This opinion does not foreclose [prevent] the District Court from concluding, upon a proper showing by the Government that meets the Government's constitutional burden as defined in this opinion, that COPA is the least restrictive alternative available to accomplish Congress' goal.

On this record, the Government has not shown that the less restrictive alternatives proposed by respondents should be disregarded. Those alternatives, indeed, may be more effective than the provisions of COPA. The District Court did not abuse its discretion when it entered the preliminary injunction. The judgment of the Court of Appeals is affirmed, and the case is remanded for proceedings consistent with this opinion.

> *"The First Amendment was designed to protect words-discourse, not pictures-arousal."*

Online Pornography Should Not Be Protected as Free Speech

Judith Reisman

In the following viewpoint, author Judith Reisman argues that pornography's potential for harm is so great that it should not be eligible for protection under the First Amendment. Citing various scientific sources, Reisman argues that pornographic images alter the brains of those who view them, including children. This alteration can lead to criminal sexual behavior. By upholding the Child Online Protection Act (COPA), these dangerous images can be stopped, she maintains. Moreover, Reisman points out, the First Amendment protects words, not images. Judith Reisman is the president of the conservative Institute for Media Education. She publishes extensively on the subject of sex education.

As you read, consider the following questions:

1. What are the two main aspects of COPA, as cited by the author?

2. According to Reisman, what do children learn by viewing pornographic pictures?

3. Who does the author call upon to "bring our laws up to speed?"

BBC Online [in 2004] reported in a "National Children's Homes" study that "[c]hild porn *crimes* have risen by 1,500% since 1988." But "Why," we ask? And why, are "over one in three [users] involved in hands-on abuse?" Is it because the human brain is designed—rigged—to *believe* that any image it sees is real, *so that millions of sexually aroused viewers act out on children the "sex" they've seen?* If yes, would that *fact* stain the "free speech" defense of pornography? This is the question we will briefly explore here. [As the March 2002 *Scientific American* reported:]

> [C]hild abuse . . . sculpts the brain to exhibit various antisocial . . . behaviors . . . violence and abuse. . . . This suggests that much more effort must be made to *prevent childhood abuse* and neglect. (Harvard neurobiologist Martin Teicher in "Scars That Won't Heal.") (Emphasis added.)

The *prevention* of "child porn crimes" leads us directly to the Child Online Protection Act (COPA). COPA . . . would criminalize commercial Web sites (1) that regularly engage in the business of selling, and (2) then knowingly make available to minors, the kind of pornography that meets the legal standard of obscene or obscene for minors.

The National Law Center for Children and Families [NLCCF] wrote the "COPA Brief of Members of Congress." The brief made legal history by unveiling recent data on how pornographic pictures re-form the human brain:

Sophisticated medical diagnostic techniques confirm that images override text for brain dominance and research indi-

Pornography by the Numbers

[The] growth of porn [on the Internet] has accelerated to a point where definitive statistics are virtually impossible to compile. Many of the numbers stretch way beyond what most of us can comprehend. Nevertheless, to give you some idea, here are some random examples. Some 200 million people are online worldwide, and studies place pornography at between 20 and 30 per cent of all Internet traffic. The only words entered in search engines more often than 'sex' are 'the' and 'and'. One study recorded 98 million visits to the top five free porn sites per month, and 19 million per month to the top five paying sites.

Decca Aitkenhead, Observer *(London), March 30, 2003.*

cates that a pornographic environment "colonizes" a viewer's brain, *producing structural changes* in the brain that are *involuntary* and can last for years. (Emphasis added.)

Pornographic pictures can cause permanent brain change. These disinhibiting images can be reawakened at any time, like it or not.

Protecting Children's Brains

Neurologists question which of the brain's hemisphere[s] will gain control of shared functions and dominate overt behavior, in light of the fact that every second millions of messages bombard the brain and carry information from the body's senses. Inhibitory transmitters help to shape the neural networks that underlie all behavior and control negative behavioral responses. There is evidence that the inhibitory health function of a minor's nervous system can be critically stressed by pornographic imagery.

Are children's minds being negatively sexualized? Are children's natural inhibitions being eroded? If so, we would expect sharp increases—post 1950—in *children's* mental, physical and sexual disorders. The COPA NLCCF brief continues:

> [H]ealth statistics indicate that a significant percentage of minors may be highly vulnerable to the toxic effect of pornographic stimuli. Researchers claim that 25 percent of the population of the United States is under age 18, and at least 12 percent of these minors have a diagnosable mental illness. Current Department of Justice data indicate that 67 percent of all sex abuse victims are minors, and of these, 34 percent are under age 11, and 14 percent are under age 5. According to an Australian study, exposure to online pornography is a "key factor" *in the increase of incidents involving young children committing sexual offenses, including "oral sex and forced intercourse," against other children.* (Emphasis added.)

This is a predictable outcome of massive sociosexual disinhibition.

The Violence and Brain Injury Institute now cites "media influences" as a "macrosocial" cause of crime and violence. Modern brain-scans provide ample evidence of how media reshapes brain, mind and memory. Sexual or violent *images* will dominate *any* text (speech).

To respond to the written word we must be able to read! Children cannot commonly *read* sex manuals but they can and do mimic sex pictures. They are taught how to molest babies and toddlers by repeating their own abuse and/or by repeating what they see—commonly in erotic pictures. The civilizing task of the "free speech" amendment is subverted when emotional right hemisphere pornography overrides the weaker left hemisphere speech tasks of logic and analysis.

"Strong responses" defines our brain's neurochemistry in action. Pornography isn't *like* a drug, it *is* a polydrug. For example, psychologist M. Douglas Reed cites just a few of many neurochemicals triggered by viewing pornography.

"Arousal dependence may be compared to biochemical alterations related to excessive amphetamine use. . . . Fantasy behaviors can be related to such neurotransmitters as dopamine, norepinephrine, or serotonin, all of which are chemically similar to the main psychedelic drugs such as LSD."

Profound Effects

Very "harmful to minors" are the spam or split-second "teaser" sex images that trigger [a] drug "high." Says neurologist Gary Lynch:

"[A]n event which lasts half a second within five to ten minutes has produced a structural change that is in some ways as profound as the structural changes one sees in [brain] damage . . . [and] can . . . leave a trace that will last for years."

No wonder a Government Accounting Office report on 550 sex offender clinics—1977 to 1996—found none had cured sex offenders. Predators re-experience an endogenous drug "high" when seeing pictures of naked or "provocative" women and/or children.

Plainly, the media cannot be blamed for all sexual wrongdoing. Yet the media must be held legally and socially accountable for its harmful, lying pictures about women and children's sexuality and their alleged lust for indiscriminate or sadistic sex. Does such brainwashing expire judicial decisions legitimizing even "virtual child pornography?" For the brain processes "virtual" child pornography as *real* "sexy children." Lynch and others documented the rigorous scientific experiments that finally established that the *brain processes what it sees as true!*

Not Protected by Free Speech Laws

Until recently most neurologists doubted the affect of media upon the national mind. Naturally we would expect a lag time until legislators and judges also understand a causal connection. The scientifically fraudulent idea that erotic images are harmless speech and children are naturally sexual has led to mass child victimization. An uninformed judiciary has subjected millions of children and youths to toxic images that now dominate their brains, minds, memories and conduct.

The First Amendment was designed to protect words-discourse, not pictures-arousal. Pornographic images neuro-chemically blitz our brains—overriding *legitimate* informed consent. Enlightened lawmakers will have to bring our laws up-to-speed with the power of media to shape our brains, minds, memories and our civility. COPA is a beginning.

> *"How can the government's [pornography] policy possibly achieve its stated goals, without creating an unprecedentedly intrusive censorship machinery?"*

Pornography Should Not Be Controlled Through Legislation

Eugene Volokh

Eugene Volokh is a law professor at UCLA. In the following viewpoint, he argues that there is no feasible way for the government to control pornography through laws without either trampling on civil liberties or spending enormous amounts of time, effort, and energy. Volokh presents three approaches the government could take in order to crack down on pornography on the Internet and shows how each would be either ineffective or oppressive. Volokh makes it clear that he does not advocate either for or against the existence of pornography but is merely concerned with protecting American civil rights.

As you read, consider the following questions:

1. What is the only potential benefit of going after U.S. pornographers, in Volokh's opinion?

Eugene Volokh, "Obscenity Crackdown—What Will the Next Step Be?" *The Volokh Conspiracy*, April 8, 2004. http://volokh.com. Reproduced by permission of the author.

2. What are "honeypot" sites, as defined by the author?

3. Name two of the three possible outcomes of the crackdown on porn, as listed by Volokh.

So here's what I wonder about the Justice Department's planned obscenity crackdown. As we know, there's lots of porn of all varieties out there on the Internet. I don't know how much of it is produced in the U.S.—but even if it's 75 percent, and every single U.S. producer is shut down, wouldn't foreign sites happily take up the slack?

It's not like Americans have some great irreproducible national skills in smut-making, or like it takes a $100 million Hollywood budget to make a porn movie. Foreign porn will doubtless be quite an adequate substitute for the U.S. market. Plus the foreign distributors might even be able to make and distribute copies of the existing U.S.-produced stock—I doubt that the imprisoned copyright owners will be suing them for infringement (unless the U.S. government seizes the copyrights, becomes the world's #1 pornography owner, starts trying to enforce the copyrights against overseas distributors, and gets foreign courts to honor those copyrights, which is far from certain and likely far from cheap).

And even if overall world production of porn somehow improbably falls by 75 percent, will that seriously affect the typical porn consumer's diet? Does it matter whether you have, say, 100,000 porn titles (and live feeds) to choose from, or just 25,000? So we have three possible outcomes:

Considering the Options

(1) The U.S. spends who knows how many prosecutorial and technical resources going after U.S. pornographers. A bunch of them get imprisoned. U.S. consumers keep using the same amount of porn as before. Maybe they can't get porn on cable channels or in hotel rooms any more, but they can get more than they ever wanted on the Internet. Nor do I think that the

crackdown will somehow subtly affect consumers' attitudes about the morality of porn—it seems highly unlikely that potential porn consumers will decide to stop getting it because they hear that some porn producers are being prosecuted.

The only potential benefit: If you really think that the porn industry is very bad for its actors, you're at least sparing Americans that harm, and shifting it off-shore instead. Other than that: The investment of major prosecutorial resources yields a net practical benefit of roughly zero.

(2) The government gets understandably outraged by the "foreign smut loophole." "Given all the millions that we've invested in going after the domestic porn industry, how can we tolerate all our work being undone by foreign filth-peddlers?," pornography prosecutors and their political allies would ask. So they unveil the solution, in fact pretty much the only solution that will work: Nationwide filtering.

It's true: Going after cyberporn isn't really that tough—if you require every service provider in the nation to block access to all sites that are on a constantly updated government-run "Forbidden Off-Shore Site" list. Of course, there couldn't be any trials applying community standards and the like before a site is added to the list; that would take far too long. The government would have to be able to just order a site instantly blocked, without any hearing with an opportunity for the other side to respond, since even a quick response would take up too much time, and would let the porn sites just move from location to location every several weeks.

Violating Free Speech?

Sure, that sounds like a violation of First Amendment procedural rules, even when the government is going after substantively unprotected obscenity. Sure, that would make it easier for the government to put all sorts of other sites on the list. Sure, it's a substantially more intrusive step than any of the Internet regulations we've seen so far, and is substantially

Better Ways to Limit Porn Exposure

I'm actually more concerned about exposure to violence on TV or video games than I am about porn popping up on [a kid's] computer screen. Certainly, in the battle of free speech versus cleaning up the Internet, there are no easy answers, at least in the sense that they can be applied fairly and uniformly. But there are a lot of solutions that work more effectively and are less insidiously destructive to civil liberties than anti-porn legislation.

For instance, I use a filter program that I monitor and update regularly. I participate with my children and watch where they go and explain why they can't buy something on the Internet or register for something with their name and address. They are not allowed to use e-mail or instant messaging unless they want to use the parental accounts while being monitored. Some parents I know also use the honor system. No filters are installed, but if the children are caught, they lose their privileges. Is all this too much work for parents? If so, then it may be time for parents to take away Internet access from the kids. As one reader of *The New York Times* put it, letting children use the Internet unsupervised is akin to dropping them off on a street corner in a strange city.

Scot Peterson, eWeek, July 12, 2004.

more intrusive in some ways than virtually any speech restriction in American history. (I say in some ways, not in all ways, since it would have a limited substantive focus—but the procedure would be unprecedently restrictive, and First Amendment law has always recognized the practical importance of procedure.) But it's the only approach that has any hope of really reducing the accessibility of porn to American consumers.

(3) Finally, the government can go after the users: Set up "honeypot" sites (seriously, that would be the technically correct name for them) that would look like normal off-shore pornography sites. Draw people in to buy the stuff. Figure out who the buyers are (you'd have to ban any anonymizer Web sites that might be used to hide such transactions by setting up some sort of mandatory filtering such as what I described in option 2). Then arrest them and prosecute them. Heck, lock each one up for several years like you would a child-porn buyer. Make him register as a sex offender. Seize his house on the theory that it's a forfeitable asset, since it was used to facilitate an illegal transaction. All because he, or he and his wife, like to get turned on by watching pictures of people having sex. Then repeat for however many people it takes to get everyone scared of the Smut Police.

So we really have three possible outcomes:

(1) The crackdown on porn is doomed to be utterly ineffective at preventing the supposedly harmful effects of porn on its viewers, and on the viewers' neighbors.

(2) The crackdown on porn will be made effective—by implementing a comprehensive government-mandated filtering system run by some administrative agency that constantly monitors the Net and requires private service providers to block any sites that the agency says are obscene.

(3) The crackdown on porn will turn into a full-fledged War on Smut that will be made effective by prosecuting, imprisoning, and seizing the assets of porn buyers.

Intrusive Censorship

Seriously I don't see many other alternatives. The government could try to put pressure on financial intermediaries; for instance, requiring Visa and MasterCard to refuse transactions with certain locations; but unless that's made just as intrusive as option #2 above, it will be hopelessly ineffective, since sites can easily just periodically change their payee names, or use various off-shore intermediaries. The government might also try to persuade foreign countries to join its campaign, but I'm pretty sure that won't work, either. First, the Europeans are apparently fairly tolerant of much porn, and, second, I highly doubt that we can persuade every poor third-world country, some of which have thriving trades in real flesh, to spend its resources creating and actually enforcing anti-porn laws, in the face of whatever payoffs the porn industry is willing to provide.

So, supporters of the Justice Department's plans, which do you prefer—#1, #2, or #3? Note that I'm not asking whether porn is bad, or whether porn should be constitutionally protected. I'm certainly not asking whether we'd be better off in some hypothetical porn-free world (just like no sensible debate about alcohol, drug, or gun policy should ask whether we'd be better off in some hypothetical alcohol-, drug-, or gun-free world).

I'm asking: How can the government's policy possibly achieve its stated goals, without creating an unprecedentedly intrusive censorship machinery, one that's far, far beyond what the Justice Department is talking about right now?

> *"To protect children from Internet pornography, education and technology (filters and monitors) and law will also be necessary."*

Legislation Can Be Helpful in Controlling Pornography

Robert Peters

In the following viewpoint, Robert Peters argues that Congress must be permitted to pass legislation that protects children from online pornography. When the Supreme Court refused to uphold the Child Online Protection Act (COPA), Peters writes, it impeded Congress's ability to govern in an effective manner. Congress is the institution best equipped to evaluate the danger of pornography, not the courts, argues Peters, and legislation such as COPA is the best way to keep Internet pornography away from children. Robert Peters is the president of the conservative nonprofit group Morality in Media, which combats obscenity on television, the Internet, and in print.

As you read, consider the following questions:

1. What does COPA prohibit, as noted by Peters?

2. What can the Supreme Court no longer be counted on to do, in the author's opinion?

3. According to Peters, what is one problem with Internet screening technology?

I would have been pleasantly surprised had the Supreme Court in *Ashcroft v. American Civil Liberties Union* upheld the Child Online Protection Act (COPA), a law intended to restrict children's access to commercial websites that distribute sex materials that are harmful to minors (i.e., obscene for minors). Minors are defined as children under age 17.

COPA prohibits the knowing posting, for commercial purposes, of World Wide Web content that is harmful to minors. Similar to the federal "dial-a-porn" law [that restricts minors' access to sex-service phone numbers], COPA provides an affirmative defense to content providers who restrict access to prohibited content by requiring a credit card or "any other reasonable measures that are feasible under available technology."

On June 29, [2005,] the Supreme Court, rather than upholding COPA, affirmed the decision of the ACLU-minded Third Circuit Court of Appeals in Philadelphia and remanded the case to the federal district court in that city to determine if there are less restrictive alternatives to COPA. In so doing, the Supreme Court noted that in the earlier proceeding granting a preliminary injunction, the "primary alternative" considered by the District Court was "blocking and filtering software.". . .

The Adverse Effects of Pornography

For those who need convincing that the *floodtide* of [pornography] pouring into our nation's communities and homes is adversely affecting children, a good place to begin is the ObscenityCrimes.org website.

For the record here, however, I do include a quote from Dr. Victor B. Cline, a clinical psychologist and Professor

Emeritus at the University of Utah, and from Dr. Mary Anne Layden, Director of Education, Center for Cognitive Therapy at the University of Pennsylvania. First, from Dr. Cline:

> Some of my porn addict patients inform me that the Internet has three major advantages in feeding their addictive sexual illnesses. . . . It's easily Accessible, Affordable and Anonymous. I have had boys in their early teens getting into this wasteland with really disastrous consequences. They told me they actively search for porn on the Internet, keying in on such words as sex, nudity, pornography, obscenity, etc. Then, once they have found how to access it, they go back again and again—just like drug addicts.

Now from Dr. Layden:

> The messages of Internet pornography are psychologically toxic, untrue, difficult to undo and are shaped by individuals whose goals are to make money without concern for the consequences. You wouldn't allow the drug pusher on the corner to come into your home, school or library and teach your child about medication. Why would you allow the sex pusher on the Internet to come into your home school or library and educate your child about sexuality? We owe it to our youth to give them the best, protect them from the worst, and to use our wisdom, education and experience to decide which is which.

Dr. Layden also noted that the pornographic images children receive "are permanently implanted in the brain and the unhealthy messages these images support are not easily talked away.". . .

Court Undermines Congress

The Supreme Court, however, can no longer be counted on to defend the home, children, considerations of decency and morality, separation of powers, or its own precedent against the relentless assaults of pornographers and radical libertarians. . . .

A Profitable, Thriving Business

The $4 billion that Americans spend on video pornography is larger than the annual revenue accrued by either the N.F.L., the N.B.A. or Major League Baseball. But that's literally not the half of it: the porn business is estimated to total between $10 billion and $14 billion annually in the United States when you toss in porn networks and pay-per-view movies on cable and satellite, Internet Web sites, in-room hotel movies, phone sex, sex toys and that archaic medium of my own occasionally misspent youth, magazines. Take even the low-end $10 billion estimate (from a 1998 study by Forrester Research in Cambridge, Mass.), and pornography is a bigger business than professional football, basketball and baseball put together. People pay more money for pornography in America in a year than they do on movie tickets, more than they do on all the performing arts combined. As one of the porn people I met in the industry's epicenter, the San Fernando Valley, put it, "We realized that when there are 700 million porn rentals a year, it can't just be a million perverts renting 700 videos each."

Frank Rich, New York Times, *May 20, 2001.*

This is not to say that Congress always gets it right, but to presume that a district court judge is better at getting it right than both Houses of Congress and the President borders on the ludicrous. I am also unaware of a Constitutional provision requiring Congress to jump through whatever evidentiary hoops the Supreme Court decides are appropriate in order to legislate. . . .

I spoke with a mother who caught her pre-teen son using the family computer—stationed in a common area—to access porn sites. The mother had not installed screening technology because, in her words, "I was naïve about the Internet; I thought you had to pay for pornography." The mother subsequently installed technology, but the damage was done. As a mother put it in a published article:

> It was a huge heartbreak for me to view the sites my son had seen. The pornographers stole my son's innocence and the horrible part is it happened in my own home! He saw more perverted sex on those sites than I have ever seen in my 51 years of living. . . .

Parental use of screening technology on home computers cannot prevent children from stumbling into Internet porn or purposefully seeking it out, when they are away from home.

Internet screening technology also does not block all porn sites. In this respect computer porn is more like the dial-a-porn (where restrictions on indecent messages were upheld) than cable porn. . . .

Congressional Law Is Necessary

The Court in *Ashcroft v. ACLU* makes much of the fact that COPA, standing alone, cannot completely protect children from Internet porn because COPA doesn't apply to websites located overseas. However Justice [Stephen] Breyer explains in his dissent, neither does screening technology, standing alone, ". . . solve the 'child protection' problem."

> Filtering software, as presently available, does not solve the 'child protection' problem. It suffers from four serious inadequacies that prompted Congress to pass the legislation instead of relying on its voluntary use. First, its filtering is faulty, allowing some pornographic material to pass through without hindrance. . . . Second, filtering costs money. Not every family has the $40 to install it. . . . Third, filtering software depends upon parents willing to decide where children will surf the web and able to enforce that decision. As to millions of American families, that is not a reasonable possibility. . . . Fourth, software blocking lacks precision, with the result that . . . it blocks a great deal of material that is valuable. . . .

Our nation's entertainment media are currently engaged in a "full court press" to curb copyright violations on the Internet-through education (which includes "educating" parents about their responsibilities) and technology and law. To protect children from Internet pornography, education and technology (filters and monitors) and law will also be necessary.

There is also something troublesome about the Supreme Court's attempt to condition the exercise of Congress's power to protect children from Internet porn on whether other nations do their part. Presumably, if the U.S. gets serious about curbing obscenity here, most other nations will do what they can to curb obscenity within their own borders. But if some other nations refuse, does that mean Congress is helpless to address the problem within U.S. borders?

If so, shouldn't the same rationale apply to the entertainment media's efforts to curb copyright violations? Clearly, much of the infringement problem is international. . . .

Clearly the Constitution, as our nation's founding fathers understood the document and as the Supreme Court itself understood it for almost 200 years, was not intended to cripple government's power to protect children or society from obscenity and indecency. As the Supreme Court noted in *Roth v. United States*, "[E]xpressions found in numerous opinions indicate that this Court has always assumed that obscenity is not protected by the freedoms of speech and press.". . .

Interpreting the First Amendment

Our nation's founding fathers viewed the First Amendment within a framework of ordered liberty—not as a license to publish pornography, to strip naked in public places for the purpose of sexually arousing patrons, or to commercially distribute material harmful to minors without any legal obligation to adopt sensible measures to restrict children's access.

Many among our nation's secular elite now espouse a radically different view of the First Amendment, and they have every right to do so. What they don't have a right to do is enlist accommodating Supreme Court Justices to effectively amend the First Amendment by means of specious decisions. The power to amend is reserved to the people and their representatives.

Admittedly, there is often a fine line between properly interpreting a Constitutional provision and in effect amending it to reflect the Justices' personal preferences or ideologies, irrespective of the history of a provision, the will of the American people, common sense and the Court's own precedent.

But if that line no longer exists and Justices can effectively amend various provisions in the Constitution to reflect the Justices' own views (and, in the process, to "sit in judgment" over a wider and wider array of legislative and executive branch functions), then ours is no longer a government of the people, by the people and for the people, as [Abraham] Lincoln aptly put it.

What we have instead is a judicial oligarchy [government by the few] accountable to no one. The official amendment process is simply too cumbersome to be an effective check on a Court that is now a law unto itself and that is ever changing the meaning of our nation's new "living" Constitution.

I would add finally that many of the Court's First Amendment problems could be avoided by the exercise of great restraint in cases involving facial challenges to necessary and reasonable laws because of perceived overbreadth or vagueness problems. Freedom of speech and press is indeed a "fundamental" right but so is the right to live and raise children in a safe, healthy and decent society. Increasingly, however, the Court's libertarian Justices foolishly ignore the warning enunciated in *Columbia Broadcasting System v. Democratic National Committee*:

"Thus, in evaluating the First Amendment claims . . . we must afford great weight to the decisions of Congress. . . . Professor [Zechariah] Chafee aptly observed: 'Once we get away from the bare words of the [First] Amendment, we must construe it as part of a Constitution which creates a government for the purpose of performing several very important tasks. The Amendment should be interpreted so as to not cripple the regular work of government.'"

> "Governments are doing their best to censor and control the Internet. . . . [and] there are growing but ineffective attempts to block pornography through legislation."

The Government Should Not Monitor the Internet to Control Pornography

Michael J. Miller

In the following viewpoint, technology writer Michael J. Miller argues that the governnment's efforts to monitor Internet use through the Child Online Protection Act (COPA) are a small but dangerous step toward censorship and an infringement on civil liberties. The Internet is a uniquely free, open, and democratic medium, Miller writes, and every effort must be made to preserve those qualities. In oppressive societies, one of the first steps governments take is restricting the Internet. Miller writes a regular column for PC Magazine, *a periodical on computing.*

Michael J. Miller, "When the Government Knows Where You Search," *PC Magazine* (Opinions), vol. 25, March 1, 2006. Copyright © 2006 Ziff Davis Publishing Holdings, Inc. All rights reserved. Reproduced by permission.

As you read, consider the following questions:

1. Why has the Bush administration asked major search engines for information on Web searches, according to the author?
2. What is one option for people who do not want to be tracked online, according to Miller?
3. What message does the author worry is being sent by the placing of minor constraints on the Internet?

I worry that even well-intentioned U.S. actions that place minor restrictions on the Internet are sending the wrong message.

Governments are doing their best to censor and control the Internet. Sometimes their goals sound lofty; sometimes they seem really sinister. But any way you look at it, the push for very open, free, and anonymous information on the Web is meeting a lot of resistance.

Just look at the U.S., where, compared with most of the world, the controls are minimal. We have laws restricting what minors are allowed to do online. There are growing but ineffective attempts to block pornography through legislation. And the government is trying to intercept more messages as part of the war against terrorism. All of these have led to controversy in recent days.

The Bush administration asked the major search engines for information on the most popular Web searches, as part of an effort to reinstate the Child Online Protection Act (COPA) [COPA was struck down by the Supreme Court in 2004]. Yahoo! and MSN complied, while Google decided to fight the order.

I'm not convinced that COPA is the right way to protect our kids online. Content filtering has gotten better over the past few years, and the big search engines block out the worst content by default. But more important, I'm concerned that the government tried to keep its requests for this search information a secret. If Google hadn't complained, we wouldn't know about it.

Despite the outcry against what Yahoo! and MSN did and what Google is fighting, it isn't really a privacy issue. The information they've been asked for isn't personally identifiable. But the reason people are getting upset is that it points out what many people don't realize—that these search engines often do keep information about individual searches.

Of course Google—or whichever major search engine you use—knows a lot about you. That's how search engines serve relevant ads. But users are rightly concerned that these engines can figure out who is searching for what—either through log-ins or IP addresses. And users often don't understand what information the search engines are collecting and how those companies are using the data.

If you want to be private, it helps to understand how companies can track you online. The easiest way is via cookies, which are simple enough to delete. IP tracking is harder to stop, but there are ways around it, through various anonymizing programs such as Anonymizer, Tenebril's GhostSurf, Tor, and the Java Anonymous Proxy. These programs do help people in repressive environments, but using them is too much trouble for the average computer user, as they add a level of complexity and delays.

For most of us, the best solution would simply be for the companies we deal with to tell us exactly what information they are collecting, what they are saving, and how they are aggregating or supplementing that data. Do companies share information among their different properties? For instance, does AOL know what shows you are watching on Time Warner video or whether you subscribe to *Sports Illustrated*? Does MSN know what versions of Windows you have registered for?

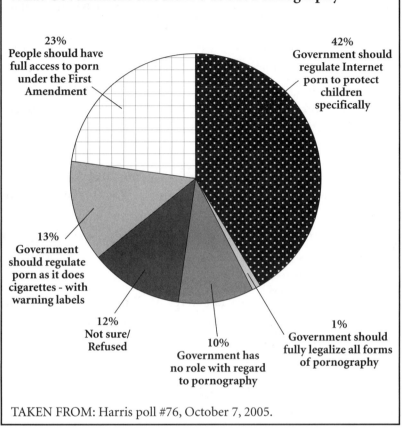

What Government Should Do about Pornography

23%
People should have full access to porn under the First Amendment

42%
Government should regulate Internet porn to protect children specifically

13%
Government should regulate porn as it does cigarettes - with warning labels

12%
Not sure/ Refused

10%
Government has no role with regard to pornography

1%
Government should fully legalize all forms of pornography

TAKEN FROM: Harris poll #76, October 7, 2005.

We need more transparent privacy policies, ones that make it much more clear what information sites collect and use. I don't mind Yahoo! keeping a cookie on my machine for its My Yahoo! page, but I may not want it to keep a log of my searches.

Giving users more control over their personal information is a goal that in the long run would serve the Web services, the government, and consumers best.

Government vs. a Free Internet

If the problem of keeping the Internet free, available, and anonymous is difficult in open and democratic societies, it's even harder in more closed societies such as China.

All the major search engines now filter their results at the behest of the Chinese government. They do so because that's "the price of doing business in China," and they typically say that in the long run having the Internet and all that information out there will facilitate a more open exchange of ideas. And China is a big market: The U.S., with 203 million users, is now the biggest market, but it's pretty much saturated. China is second, with 103 million users—less than 8 percent of its population.

Google is the latest to give in. Until recently, it didn't have a Chinese site. The Chinese government blocks a number of political sites, but users could at least find out they existed using Google and then try to circumvent the restrictions. But now Google has a Chinese site that eliminates the sites the government doesn't want its citizens to see.

There are no great answers here. A Chinese journalist was jailed after Yahoo! turned over his e-mails. Microsoft has blocked antigovernment blogs all over the world, and it's still doing so in China.

It's not just search engines that are a concern. All sorts of tech companies make products that can be used for repression: databases that can keep track of what people are doing, firewalls that can block certain sites, and routers that can monitor what people are doing online. It's fruitless to say that U.S. tech companies shouldn't participate in the Chinese market, but what they could do is at least fight for more transparency there—and it would be good to see them come together to suggest proper rules.

China isn't the only country restricting the Internet. The U.S. has rules aimed at protecting minors. A number of European countries have restrictions against Nazi or racist content. But these are nothing compared with closed societies. One of the first things the new hard-line Iranian government did was crack down on the Web.

Even the U.S. government's asking Yahoo! and Google for large amounts of data makes people more careful with their searches. I worry that even well-intentioned actions to place minor constraints on the Internet are sending a message that restricting information is acceptable. In one sense, the countries that make finding dissident sites close to impossible are pushing that message to an extreme. And that's a bad sign for all of us.

Becoming a Blogger

I'm a little late to the party, but I've recently started a new Forward Thinking blog. I've been writing stories for the Web for a long time, and technically have had another blog that mostly repurposed my Miller's Choice newsletter, a collection of links to my favorite Ziff Davis stories of the week. But our software has gotten better, and I have a little more time these days, so I thought I'd try my hand at writing a real blog that covers my opinions of the conferences I attend and the new products I see.

I've tried this out first at eg2006—Richard Saul Wurman's eclectic and fascinating "entertainment gathering"—and at DEMO '06, the annual launch pad for a whole range of new products. It's been an interesting experience. I do find myself scrambling to write about all the things I see, and I find that sometimes I don't do as much research as I normally would. But I'm writing more freely about more topics and I can post much more quickly. No copy editors and no Web producers; just me, the blog, and an Internet connection. Check it out at http://blog.pcmag.com/miller and let me know what you think.

> "In a world of online social networking, decentralized networks and servers, and increasingly tech-savvy child predators, it's going to take a united effort among government, industry, and families to keep [children] safe."

The Government Should Have a Role in Monitoring Pornography on the Internet

J. Nicholas Hoover

J. Nicholas Hoover is an associate editor at Information Week *magazine who writes about networking and government policy. In the following viewpoint, Hoover outlines the dangers of unregulated social networking sites and pornographic Web sites and argues that the government, as well as industry and family, should work to protect children from sexual predators on these sites. Hoover supports Justice Department monitoring and crackdowns on potential predators; these limits come with the benefit of child protection, he writes. There are other ways to protect children—installing filters, for instance—but only the government has the reach and funds to provide wide-scale Internet monitoring.*

As you read, consider the following questions:

1. In addition to communities for young people to interact with, what else have social sites become, according to the author?

2. What is one trick named by Hoover that child pornographers use to conceal their identities online?

3. What is the name of the Justice Department's effort to combat child exploitation on the federal, state, and local levels, as cited by the author?

Given his lurid obsessions, you'd think Rich would want to hide, but his profile at social networking site MySpace .com includes not only information about himself but also an e-mail address for future correspondence.

Most of the 305 contacts listed on Rich's MySpace page claim to be kids—"claim" because the identities of strangers in cyberspace are hard to verify. In their own MySpace profiles, several of the kids responding to Rich are posing in their underwear; one says he's an 11-year-old who sneaked by MySpace's age controls by claiming to be 18.

MySpace and social networking sites like it offer thriving communities where young people engage in countless hours of banal chatter and photo sharing. Not coincidentally, social sites also have become hangouts for child predators, child pornographers, and other lowlifes.

It's a high-risk dynamic with potentially terrible consequences. In February [2006], the naked, strangled body of 14-year-old Judy Cajuste was found in a New Jersey trash bin, and the body of 15-year-old Kayla Reed was discovered in a California canal. In both cases, investigators are probing possible connections to MySpace: Cajuste had told friends of meeting a 20-something man there, and Reed logged into her MySpace account the day before she disappeared. There are dozens of other examples of young people lured into "friendships" that put them in danger.

Several teens we talked to acknowledged their peers could be susceptible to come-ons from strangers. "It happens," says a 16-year-old girl. "You're a young girl, and people compliment you. You're more willing to meet them."

MySpace, in an effort to better protect its millions of young members, just hired its first chief security officer. Hemanshu Nigam, . . . played a central role in online safety at Microsoft until being hired by MySpace. Before that, he chased down child predators as a U.S. prosecutor.

Teenagers Are Vulnerable

Tech-savvy kids, with their cell phones, instant messaging accounts, and access to PCs at home and school, are targets for sexual predators. Too many of them are ready and willing to share personal information online without a thought to how it might be misused by others. The National Center for Missing and Exploited Children reports that one in five kids online has been solicited or enticed. Reports of child pornography on the center's CyberTipline have increased six of the last seven years [from 1999 to 2006].

"The threat is frighteningly real, it is growing rapidly, and it must be stopped," U.S. Attorney General Alberto Gonzales said [in April 2006] in a speech at the center. (Gonzales provided graphic descriptions of child pornography to get his point across.) Gonzales noted that the tools of the predator trade have made it harder to investigate and bring criminal charges.

Funding for a network of 46 police task forces set up by the federal government's Internet Crimes Against Children program has more than doubled to $14 million annually, and the [George W.] Bush administration sent legislation to Congress to increase penalties if Internet service providers find but fail to report child pornography on their systems.

Private industry also is getting more involved. The Financial Coalition Against Child Pornography, started in March

[2006], includes financial and Internet companies working with law enforcement and the Center for Missing and Exploited Children to identify child pornographers and stop them from using banks, credit cards, and Internet payment systems. AOL has worked with law enforcers since a 1995 investigation revealed child porn being traded in its chat rooms, and Yahoo regularly pulls message boards where the illicit material gets shared off its site. Microsoft helped law enforcers develop collaboration software called the Child Exploitation Tracking System, has sponsored the training of 1,300 police officers on child porn, and said it would provide the U.K.-based Internet Watch Foundation with more than $500,000 worth of free software. CA [Computer Associates] and Sun Microsystems have donated money and resources to the Center for Missing and Exploited Children.

Business and technology professionals may think of online child safety as a family issue, but it's a workplace issue, too. Five states—Arkansas, Missouri, Oklahoma, South Carolina, and South Dakota—require IT [information technology] technicians to report child pornography if they come across it, and others are considering such measures.

Pornography in the Workplace

Social networks aren't just a teen phenomenon. A survey by Web filtering company Websense found that 8% of respondents visit social networking sites while at work. Companies can use Web filters to limit access to the sites, though Websense says its customers don't seem overly concerned.

Whiling away company time on social networks is a productivity issue; luring children for sex is a criminal one. There's little evidence that sexual predators are trolling from workplace PCs, but it's been known to happen. In 2003, a Cincinnati-area police chief admitted to soliciting sex from someone he thought was a 15-year-old, using his work computer. And a deputy press secretary at the Department of

Homeland Security, arrested in March [2006] for attempting to seduce a child, had his workplace computer seized as part of the investigation and gave the number to his government-issued cell phone to a police officer posing as a 14-year-old girl.

Child porn stored on company PCs and servers has been a bigger problem. Filtering and blocking can help keep the images off networks, though it's not fail-safe. Keyword and URL-based filters have spotty coverage. Other software scans images for limbs and skin tones and blocks pictures it identifies as porn, but skin often takes up too little of the photographs, and innocuous material can be inadvertently blocked.

Tricks of the Trade

Child predators and pornographers have tricks to conceal their identities online. One of the most common is lying about their ages, claiming to be younger than they are. To hide their IP [Internet protocol] addresses and locations, they piggyback on Wi-Fi [wireless Internet] connections or use proxy servers. Decentralized peer-to-peer networks prevent material from being tracked to a specific server, and encryption lets them keep online chats private from those policing the Web. When law enforcement, ISPs [Internet Service Providers] and others take down pedophile Web sites, it's not long before they're back up, hosted by a different service.

Guys like Rich are tough to fight. [Parry] Aftab, an attorney who runs child protection site WiredSafety.org, has worked with MySpace to develop its privacy and law enforcement policy and says site administrators surely would take Rich's profile down if they knew of it. MySpace declined to be interviewed for this story, but a spokesperson responded by e-mail that MySpace has worked with law enforcement since its inception. But with the site's ratio of 73 million users to 100 customer service personnel, investigating and responding to every complaint takes time. Profiles like Rich's put law enforc-

An Effective Weapon for Law Enforcement

When police arrested Louis Dec for molesting a 15-year-old boy, they discovered what may have been the fuel that fed his perversion.

The Cleveland resident had been downloading child pornography from the Internet and storing it on computer disks. So Cuyahoga County prosecutors had a chance to charge Dec not only with the molestation, but also to find a law that fit the high-tech pornography crime.

The perfect choice was an 18-year-old law against pandering sexual material to children.

While legislators try to update the state's laws for a digital age, prosecutors and police have found that their best weapons are already on the books.

Old laws are just as effective on the Internet, particularly when it comes to sex crimes, as anything today's lawmakers have concocted.

Chris Seper, Cleveland (OH) Plain Dealer *October 6, 2002.*

ers in a quandary, too: Even though he claims to be 37 and talks about wanting sex with boys, arguably his speech is protected by the First Amendment as he isn't specific about whether he's acting on his fantasies.

Combating Online Pornography

The Justice Department's Project Safe Childhood will seek to get law enforcement agencies at the federal, state, and local levels working together to investigate and prosecute child exploitation crimes. That also means arming law enforcers with information gleaned from ISPs, and possibly forcing them to retain data much longer than they do. The Justice Department gathered information from a group of ISPs about how people were conducting searches to find porn online—including the legal, adult variety—in its efforts to reinstate the Child Online Protection Act, a 1998 law struck down by a federal judge that was intended to shield kids from inappropriate material by, among other things, requiring people who access porn sites to prove they're of legal age. (The American Civil Liberties Union and others argued that the law violated consumer privacy.) The Justice Department, emboldened by its efforts to get ISPs to comply with its first request, has indicated it wants them to keep records of Web activity on hand longer for future requests.

The Internet Crimes Against Children program [in 2005] investigated 2,329 cases of enticement and of predators traveling to meet minors, and 252,000 cases of child pornography. Yet those numbers provide just a glimpse of the activity, since many local police forces are too small to investigate child porn. "It's absolutely overwhelming," says Brad Russ, director of Internet Crimes Against Children's training and technical assistance program, which trains 1,000 officers each year. "The scope and the scale of the problem far exceeds our capacity." Intensifying the epidemic is that more than half the world has no laws dealing with child pornography.

But police keep trying. In March [2006], two men were arrested in the first federal cases involving child predators on MySpace, and federal law enforcers shut down a site streaming live sexual abuse of toddlers, charging 27 people with child pornography. The 45 U.S. task forces made 1,623 arrests and identified 275 victims of child porn [in 2005]. Those charged or convicted as predators and child porn peddlers have been found in all walks of life, including schoolteachers and cops.

Vigilantes and Filters

Vigilante groups are fighting back. In January [2006], NBC's *Dateline* featured a report about one such group, Perverted-

Justice.org, which set up a sting that resulted in 51 men being busted in three nights. The group hasn't seen one acquittal from those it's helped bring to justice, and nearly all of its work is done with law enforcement Bryce Clayton's blog, called The Dead Kids of MySpace, and another called MyCrimeSpace post news of recent cases involving MySpace and child predators and pornography. "Just today, I came across a half-naked 13-year-old girl posing on her bed, a 15-year-old girl whose profile picture is that of her taking a bong hit . . . and numerous other underage [kids] who have posted cell numbers on their MySpace," Clayton says.

Yet some in law enforcement are wary of such efforts. "We certainly take any information that anyone has regarding an offender," says Randy Newcomb, an investigator with the New York State Police in Canandaigua, N.Y. However, vigilantes expose themselves to liability for entrapment or possession of child porn and might not properly maintain digital evidence, Newcomb says.

Putting filtering and monitoring software on kids' computers provides some protection. SearchHelp's Sentry line, for example, blocks Web sites based on keywords and creates a log of visited sites. It also lets parents and other guardians monitor a child's activity from other computers. Parents can be notified of violations via E-mail or cell phone. Sentry also monitors IM [instant messaging] conversations, using expertise culled from law enforcement to flag phrases commonly used by predators.

Any IT pro knows of the limitations of such tools. The filters don't work perfectly, and even if kids post and browse safely, social networking sites present a new set of problems. Profiles on the sites often link to other online information sources, providing the type of data a fixated predator might use to locate a child, such as a school name, says Michelle Collins, a unit director at the National Center for Missing and Exploited Children.

Sites Attempt to Block Predators

In addition to MySpace, Friendster.com, Facebook.com, My-Yearbook.com, and social blogging sites like Xanga.com let users post pictures, videos, and blogs, and they support E-mail and instant messaging. They're hugely successful. MySpace, purchased by [media magnate] Rupert Murdoch [in 2005] for $580 million, has grown from 6 million users to 73 million in less than a year and is the fourth most popular English-language site on the Web. Some music groups sell tickets to their concerts largely based on word of mouth at MySpace. Friendster gets 9 million hits a month, and Facebook's 7.5 million users generate the seventh largest number of page views on the Web. MySpace and Facebook have even become verbs in the mold of Google: To MySpace someone means to look at a profile or send a message.

But kids aren't always on their best behavior on these sites, with threats and cyberbullying among the problems. Some schools block social networking sites from school computers.

[In 2005], in an effort to shield younger kids from predators, MySpace stipulated that 14- and 15-year-olds can have only "private" profiles, meaning someone can't view them without their permission. A persistent cookie tells kids younger than 14 to come back when they're older. Users can set their profiles to prevent being contacted from those who don't know their last names. The site also introduced a method by which anyone finding inappropriate content can report it to administrators with one click.

More recently, MySpace created a set of public service announcements with the Center for Missing and Exploited Children. Nearly a third of the company's 300 employees work in customer service, which has deleted 250,000 underage profiles since the site's 2003 inception and filters out nudity and obscenity when found. . . .

Networking Sites Aimed at Minors

But as Rich's profile indicates, there's more to do. Anyone can join, the site's default privacy controls are set so anyone can send messages to users, and it's easy to fool the system. One teen interviewed by *InformationWeek* said his 12-year-old brother established a profile on MySpace by lying about his age.

Friendster soon will have five employees working in member services, who will seek and remove questionable content and monitor the network. Yet such a small group can't scrutinize every photograph. To maintain a level of safety, Friendster has made it so users must know first and last names to befriend others and can dictate who can see their pages and message them.

Facebook users must have valid college or high school E-mail addresses, though recently selected companies have been allowed to join. Some high schools have their own domain names, and there's a protracted process by which students at schools without their own Web sites can join, and alumni aren't allowed. When teens post information, it's only public to verified friends, not the entire Web. Children aren't at high risk of receiving messages from strangers, because it's difficult to contact a user if you don't know their name.

Because of these controls, Facebook has seen few child predators, chief privacy officer Chris Kelly says. "This has been a deliberate design choice for us," Kelly says. "We're trying to re-create the way people share information in the real world. The idea to share all that information over the open Internet struck us as sort of a silly vision."

Some sites go a step further. Jeanette Symons founded Imbee.com, a place for 8- to 14-year-olds to socialize. It includes a range of parental controls, and published material is eventually deleted so that kids don't have to worry about content coming back to haunt them—for example, when a future employer runs a background check five years down the road.

Parents are able to approve or deny online buddies and can control the scope of interaction between kids through direct communications with site administrators and without needing their kids' passwords or log-in names. Similar sites are in the works, including YFly, co-founded by teen heartthrob Nick Lachey. Still, even Symons admits there are ways to fool Imbee's system.

Parents can find the sites a rude awakening. "For 10 years, people have been saying, 'It's not my kid,'" Aftab says. But now, on sites like MySpace and Xanga, parents are seeing what kids have been saying all along in instant messages and E-mails, "and they're freaked."

Investigator Newcomb, spoke to an auditorium of elementary schoolers in western New York. He asked kids in the audience how many of them had more than 200 friends on their online buddy list—a bunch of hands shot up. Out of those, he asked how many have only friends on that list they can put a face to, and half of the hands remained raised. Finally, he asked if any of the kids had ever gone and met someone they'd got to know online, and a few hands were raised. "That's just totally frightening to me," Newcomb says. "The superintendent looked like his eyes were going to pop out of his head."

It may take a village to raise a child. But in a world of online social networking, decentralized networks and servers, and increasingly tech-savvy child predators, it's going to take a united effort among government, industry, and families to keep them safe.

Periodical Bibliography

The following articles have been selected to supplement the diverse view presented in this chapter.

Taylor Boas	"Weaving the Authoritarian Web," *Current History*, December 2004.
Linda Chavez	"Court Protects Porn, Not Political Speech," *Human Events*, July 5, 2004.
Drew Clark	"High Court Skeptical About Child Internet Protection Act," *Congress Daily*, March 5, 2003.
Lyle Denniston	"Supreme Court Revisits Arguments in Online Pornography Case," *Boston Globe*, March 3, 2004.
Jennifer A. Dlouhy	"Ruling Suggests an Alternative for Online Pornography Law," *CQ Weekly*, July 3, 2004.
Marilyn Geewax	"High Court Blocks Online Porn Law," *Atlanta Journal-Constitution*, June 30, 2004.
Katie Hafner	"After Subpoenas, Internet Searches Give Some Pause," *New York Times*, January 25, 2006.
Mary Minow	"Who Pays for Free Speech?" *American Libraries*, February 2003.
Neil Munro	"Under Pressure on Internet Porn," *National Journal*, July 19, 2003.
David Post and Bradford C. Brown	"Confusion Reigns Where Law Meets Cyberspace," *InformationWeek*, June 24, 2002.
Jeffrey Rosen	"The End of Obscenity," *New Atlantis*, Summer 2004.
Sarah Stirland	"Supreme Court: Anti-Porn Law Likely Violates Free Speech," *Congress Daily*, June 29, 2004.
Ken Walker	"Court Guts Porn Law," *Christianity Today*, September 2004.

Should Children Be Protected from Online Pornography?

Chapter Preface

Any discussion about the issue of online pornography inevitably includes some mention of children. While adults are generally free to buy and view pornography, the exposure of children to such material is a far more complicated topic. At the heart of the discussion is the question of the best way to guide children's minds. One set of beliefs holds that children need to be protected from obscene material; they should not view it or come into contact with it at all, this school of thought states. It is the duty of various authority figures—the government, the schools, parents—and even the pornography purveyors themselves to shield children from pornographic images and text, many believe.

Various conservative political and social groups frequently fall into this category. One such group is the conservative Christian organization Focus on the Family. At the organization's Web site, the group tells parents that they must protect their children. "The sheer vastness of the media boggles the mind," the group acknowledges. But nonetheless, parents must maintain "a willingness to filter the media that come into their home . . . an understanding of the values and traditions they want to impart to their kids . . . [and] a desire to safeguard young hearts and minds from images and voices that threaten those values."

Another set of beliefs centers around the idea that children should be exposed to a variety of information and concepts in a safe, controlled environment with an adult to help them place new ideas in context. This can include pornography. Those who hold these beliefs tend to be more socially and politically liberal. These individuals usually believe that prohibiting children from seeing *any* pornography makes it even more intriguing to them. It is best to let children see how degrading pornography can be so that they will avoid it on their own.

Massachusetts Institute of Technology professor Henry Jenkins told an Australian radio interviewer that this can be hard for parents, who are "caught in the middle, trying to muddle through, making the decisions day by day." He argues that exposure to pornography is a normal part of adolescence: "Most of the people of my generation had access to a *Playboy* [magazine] growing up. . . . Yes there is a risk there of access . . . to pornography [but] it's a risk that has been overstated by people who assume that any exposure is going to lead kids down a dangerous path."

For some, pornography is invasive and infectious. Children can be harmed just by seeing it, these individuals believe. For others, pornography can be a harmless and even a safe form of sexual expression for adolescents. These views and others will be explored more fully in the viewpoints of this chapter.

> *"The Internet is probably the most dangerous threat to your children ... because ... your child has instant access to the most perverted materials imaginable."*

Children Must Be Protected from Online Pornography

Frank York and Jan LaRue

Frank York is a former editor for the conservative Christian organization Focus on the Family. Jan LaRue is the chief counsel for Concerned Women for America, a conservative family-values advocacy group. In the following viewpoint, excerpted from a book York and LaRue wrote together, the authors argue that pornography is a pernicious, pervasive force in America and a particular danger to children. Children must be protected from all forms of pornography at all costs, they argue, and the Internet is a particularly dangerous place. Predators, pedophiles, and pornographers are online everywhere, in chat rooms and on Web sites. This should be a major concern for parents, the authors contend.

As you read, consider the following questions:

1. What is one specific problem that can result from children being exposed to pornography, according to the authors?

2. What is one benefit of the Internet, in York and LaRue's opinion?

3. What do the authors name as "the most dangerous threat to your children?"

Even in our Western culture that is increasingly tolerant of all things sexual, there's still a recognition among most people—whether Christian or not—that pornography is inherently bad or improper. But is it really harmful to individuals or society? After all, many men have seen a racy magazine or movie at some time and are hardly sex addicts by most definitions, let alone sexual criminals. Isn't it just a part of "Boys will be boys"? Groups like the American Civil Liberties Union and the American Library Association even defend porn vigorously as constitutionally protected free speech.

So, is pornography truly something that should have parents concerned? In a word, *yes*.

As you will soon see, children are being exposed to porn earlier than ever. And when they're exposed at whatever age, their thinking can be terribly distorted and their emotions damaged. They can become addicted and, in extreme cases, start acting out what they've seen. There's also the growing danger that they will be harmed by someone else whose own thoughts and actions have been corrupted by pornography. . . .

But just for starters, consider the following:

Effects of Pornography

Dr. Mark Laaser, executive director and cofounder of the Christian Alliance for Sexual Recovery (and himself a former porn addict), reported to a committee of the U.S. Congress, "Pornography has the ability, according to all psychological theory, to program children early. We are now seeing research that is telling us that, whereas in my generation of men, the average age a person first saw pornography was age 11, now it's age five. A child who has the ability, and we're teaching them in school to do this, can get into these [Internet porn] sites very easily—four, five, six, seven year olds now are seeing things that in my extensive history with pornography I never saw. Pornography that is being seen is violent. It is degrading. It humiliates people, and it's teaching our children very immature, immoral, and damaging roles about themselves.

"All psychological theory would certainly confirm that this kind of material, even if it's in its softest form, has the ability to affect a child's attitude, sexual orientation, and sexual preferences for the rest of their life. Internet pornography also can become very addictive. Addiction is progressive, and leads to more destructive forms of sexual acting out later in life."

A 1999 survey conducted by the Yankelovich polling firm discovered that more than 50 percent of teens admit to visiting pornography Web sites. Of the teens surveyed, a staggering 79 percent said they had found porn on their school or library computer. This figure is up 70 percent from 1997—just two years earlier. In addition, 67 percent said they access porn at home, and 64 percent said they also used a computer at a friend's house to access porn sites.

Parental Ignorance

One of the most serious statistics from this study is that 75 percent of *parents* who were surveyed claimed that they knew "everything" or a "fair amount" about what their kids were looking at on the Internet. *That reveals a glaring ignorance on the part of parents about what their children are actually seeing on the Web.*

Children are also being hustled for sex by predators who stalk the Net. In June 2000, the National Center for Missing and Exploited Children released "Online Victimization: A Report on the Nation's Youth." The survey of 5,001 youth found that 19 percent of 10- to 17-year-olds reported getting unwanted sexual advances on the Net in the year preceding. It is believed that 48 percent of these cybersex advances were made by persons *younger* than 18. Sixty-six percent of those reporting a sexual advance were female. Seventy percent of the incidents occurred when the child was at home on his computer; 65 percent occurred while the youth was in a chat room; 24 percent came from an instant message.

In addition, 25 percent of those in the "Online Victimization" survey said they had received "unwanted exposure to pictorial images of naked people or people having sex." The study says this represents an estimated 5.4 to 6.4 million children. Of the unwanted exposures, 71 percent occurred while the child was searching or surfing the Net, and 28 percent happened when opening an E-mail or clicking on links in an E-mail. Sixty-five percent of these incidents occurred at home, 15 percent in schools, and 3 percent in libraries. . . .

Benefits of the Web

The Internet is a marvel of the twentieth century, an amazing educational tool that has connected the entire world. It gives every person who owns or otherwise has access to a computer the ability to obtain information on a scale never before imagined. While television long held the distinction of being the premier communication tool in history, it is quickly being edged out by the Internet. Why? Because it provides endless choices to the user. With millions of Internet users on the planet, each one now has the ability to construct his or her own Web site and have an equal voice in communicating to the world. A reporter such as Matt Drudge, who operates out of an office in Miami, can compete on an equal footing with NBC, CBS, ABC, and Fox in the rapid dissemination of news.

A Comparison to War

One of the lessons of the 20th century was that we need to learn how to fight the "next war" instead of just learning the lessons of the last one. Technology and tactics are always changing and so are the methods and tactics of war.

The same principle holds true for threats to our children here at home. Child predators are constantly seeking new ways to update their tactics, finding new means of attacking and exploiting kids. The fight against child predators is an important one we dare not lose.

When Congress passed the "Amber Alert" bill, which was designed to help authorities recover missing and exploited children, it underscored this nation's resolve to protect its most cherished natural resource—our children. While that legislation addressed the "real" world, threats posed online in the "cyber world" are just as real.

These threats go beyond children walking to school or being alone on a playground. They penetrate the safety and sanctity of our homes and schools. They are the next war on our children, a war that is already upon us.

Joseph R. Pitts, "Protecting Our Children Online,"
May 2004. www.house.gov/pitts.

In fact, one benefit of the Internet is that for the first time in many years, political conservatives, evangelical Christians, and other "politically incorrect" individuals can communicate to the world without being filtered by liberal news sources. No longer do we find ourselves restricted by the liberal media gatekeepers who have long refused to allow conservative or evangelical viewpoints to be heard.

Dangers of the Web

Along with its benefits, however, the Internet also has its dark side. Pornographers, [reproductive rights organization]

Planned Parenthood, and other purveyors of sexual immorality are using the Net to spread their ideas. The pornographers see your child as a potential consumer of pornographic materials, and they know that if they can get your child hooked, he or she may well become a lifelong customer. With annual worldwide pornography profits estimated to be $56 billion, it doesn't take a rocket scientist to understand that this is a lucrative business.

While pornography is mainly about greed, money, and lust, it's also about an immoral and anti-Christian philosophy that can determine the direction your child will take in life. Porn changes the brain chemistry of the user, and the person who constantly feeds this addiction can end up with serious problems. He can also become a threat to others as he begins to act out his uncontrollable sexual desires.

The Internet is probably the most dangerous threat to your children. Why? Because if your home is online, your child has instant access to the most perverted materials imaginable—bestiality; transgenders, or "she/males" (men and women who are undergoing sex-change operations); homosexuality; pedophilia; and other forms of sexual perversion. Also available are "voyeur" sites featuring college co-eds who set up video cameras in their showers and bedrooms so porn addicts can view them from the privacy of their own homes. With all that just a mouse click or two away, children can become sexually addicted far faster today than they could in the days before the Internet.

The Chat Room/Forum Threat

A chat room is a place on the Web where people can discuss their interests with others in "real time." In real time, you communicate instantly with other people. It's like being on the phone, but you're using the keyboard to communicate instead of a handset. There can be dozens of people in one chat room, carrying on a conversation.

Thousands of these chat rooms exist, and many are devoted to discussions of perverted sex. Women are increasingly getting involved in affairs with men they meet in these electronic rooms. In one case, a number of women were allegedly lured to their deaths by a man they met in sadomasochistic chat rooms. Pedophiles also lurk in these rooms, as well as young male predators who enjoy engaging in cybersex or actually seducing girls online.

The same threat exists in Internet forums. These are areas where individuals can post notes to each other. It isn't done in real time as in a chat room, but people can communicate rapidly by posting messages back and forth.

Sadly, the danger to children from pornography isn't just from sources "out there," outside the home. It often comes from within one's own family or circle of friends and relatives. While a vigilant mother is doing everything she can to protect her child from pornography on the Internet or in the mass media, family members or friends may be harboring a secret addiction that threatens the safety of her son or daughter.

> "[We] ought to be sure that real, not just symbolic, harm results from youthful pursuit of disapproved pleasures and messages before mandating indecency laws, Internet filters, and other restrictive regimes."

Children Should Not Always Be Protected from Online Pornography

Marjorie Heins

In the following viewpoint, Marjorie Heins makes the argument that protecting children from various "offensive materials," including online pornography, does not help them. On the contrary, Heins writes, censoring materials for children and teenagers does them a disservice by not allowing them to form their own opinions about things they will encounter in adult life. Children should not be restricted from seeing pornography, Heins states, but instead should be taught to deal with difficult, unpleasant material in a manner consistent with good values. Marjorie Heins is a civil liberties attorney and creator of the American Civil Liberties Union's Arts Censorship Project.

Marjorie Heins, from *Not in Front of the Children: "Indecency," Censorship, and the Innocence of Youth*. Rutgers University Press, 2007. Copyright © 2001 by Marjorie Heins. All rights reserved. Reproduced by permission of the author.

As you read, consider the following questions:

1. Who are the most frequent targets of censorship, according to the author?
2. Heins states that her argument is *not* that commercial pornography is good for children. What *is* her argument?
3. According to the author, why do older children and adolescents need access to information and ideas?

A young person cannot judge what is allegorical and what is literal; anything that he receives into his mind at that age is likely to become indelible and unalterable; and therefore it is most important that the tales which the young first hear should be models of virtuous thoughts.

In 1998, citing this famous passage from Plato's *Republic* judges on the U.S. Court of Appeals rejected the legal claims of a high school drama teacher who had been punished for choosing a controversial play called *Independence* for her advanced acting class. (The play addressed themes of divorce, homosexuality, and unwed pregnancy.) The judges ruled that school officials in North Carolina did not violate Margaret Boring's right to academic freedom when they revoked her advanced acting assignment and exiled her to a middle school in response to complaints about the play. . . .

In Congress, meanwhile, the zeal to protect youth was manifested in a series of laws restricting "indecency" on television and the Internet and censoring sex education. As part of its massive 1996 welfare reform, Congress appropriated $250 million for local sex ed programs—but only if they preached abstinence until marriage and taught that any "sexual activity outside of the context of marriage is likely to have harmful psychological and physical effects." Under this "abstinence till marriage" curriculum, potentially lifesaving information on safer sex and contraception was suppressed, on the theory that

Government Get Out:
A Libertarian Opinion

In the name of "protecting children," policymakers often-times end up treating us all like juveniles. The conservative groups and political leaders that are encouraging [a] re-newed censorship crusade need to start taking their own first principles of personal responsibility and parental decision-making more seriously.

Adam Thierer, TechKnowledge, *July 6, 2001. www.cato.org.*

even learning about such subjects would lead youngsters to believe that sexual activity was encouraged.

Censorship in the name of child protection was not always solemn or health-threatening, however; sometimes it was simply comic. In 1996, the Bad Frog Brewery applied to the New York State Liquor Authority for permission to market its designer beer, with a label that featured "a frog with the second of its four unwebbed 'fingers' extended in a manner evocative of a well known human gesture of insult." The Liquor Authority rejected Bad Frog's application, largely because it felt the label could have "adverse effects" on "children of tender age." A federal trial judge agreed that the Authority had a legitimate interest in "protecting children" from "profane" advertising.

Need to Protect Minors

This exercise in government-enforced etiquette was eventually reversed, but not because the appellate judges questioned the underlying assumption that minors would be harmed by seeing the frog's crude gesture on a grocery label. To the contrary, the judges recited what had by then become a truism in U.S. constitutional law—that states have "a compelling interest in protecting the physical and psychological well-being of minors," an interest that includes shielding them from "the influence of literature that is not obscene by adult standards." The only reason for a First Amendment violation in the *Bad Frog* case, according to the appellate court, was that given "the wide currency of vulgar displays throughout contemporary society, including comic books targeted directly at children," the Liquor Authority's ban amounted to removing only a few insignificant "grains of offensive sand from a beach of vulgarity." In essence, it appeared, New York's problem was that it had not taken more *extensive* steps to censor advertising and other expression in the interest of protecting youth.

The *Bad Frog* judges never indicated why they thought exposure to the beer label would be psychologically harmful. But clearly they were acting on widely shared beliefs about harm to minors from art, literature, advertising, and other forms of communication. The assumption was that even if coarse entertainment or provocative materials are tolerable for adults, children and adolescents either are too fragile to handle vulgarity, sex, and controversy or lack the intellectual freedom rights that the First Amendment grants adults—or both.

Of course, the assumption that minors are harmed by reading, watching movies, or surfing the Internet is usually framed in terms of gratuitous violence or pornography, not controversial works of theater, silly beer labels, or novels by John Steinbeck and Toni Morrison. But terms like "pornography" and "gratuitous violence" are elastic, and if the underlying philosophy is one of protection through censorship, then it is only a matter of opinion whether gratuitous violence means *Schindler's List* or *Terminator 2*, whether safer-sex films that illustrate the unrolling of a condom are salutary or immoral, or whether Judy Blume novels that discuss masturbation or premarital sex are pornographic. Even if adults could agree, moreover, on what is truly inadvisable for young people, the rarely asked question remains, In what sense is it harmful? And does it justify censorship?

Train Children Properly

I became intrigued by these questions during my tenure as director of the American Civil Liberties Union's Arts Censorship Project (1991–98). Not only were children and teenagers the most frequent targets of censorship in these years, but they became the justification for restrictions that affected adults as well. Thus, we saw Internet rating and filtering installed on public library computers; stores refusing to carry popular music that contained warning labels; and laws prohibiting "indecency" on cable television. . . .

The continued popularity of censorship designed to protect, shield, indoctrinate, or socialize young people dramatized the durability and emotional power of the belief that minors are harmed by sexual expression—or, depending upon ones values, by speech about violence, drugs, alcohol, suicide, religion, racism, or other troublesome themes. Unexamined assumptions continue to dominate this debate, with questionable consequences not only for the First Amendment freedoms of all of us but for the moral and intellectual development of youngsters themselves. . . .

The argument here is not that commercial pornography, mindless media violence, or other dubious forms of entertainment are good for youngsters or should be foisted upon them. Rather, it is that, given the overwhelming difficulty in even defining what it is we want to censor, and the significant costs of censorship to society and to youngsters themselves, we ought to be sure that real, not just symbolic, harm results from youthful pursuit of disapproved pleasures and messages before mandating indecency laws, Internet filters, and other restrictive regimes. Perhaps there are better ways to socialize children—among them, training in media literacy and critical thinking skills, comprehensive sexuality education, literature classes that *deal with* difficult topics rather than pretending they do not exist, and inclusion of young people in journalism and policymaking on this very issue of culture and values.

In all of these areas, youngsters who are economically and educationally deprived are likely to benefit most from additional sources of information and ideas.

Harm of Censorship

Which leads to a final theme . . . the intellectual freedom interests of young people themselves. This is a concept too often impatiently dismissed by child protectionists. Minors are thought sufficiently mature or socialized to understand and resist the ideas that a majority of adults think are not good for them—or, as one federal court put it, youngsters' access to speech must be restricted lest they "get lost in the marketplace of ideas." But is this really the best way to prepare youngsters for adult life in a democratic society? The simultaneous titillation, anxiety, and confusion spawned by forbidden speech zones may do more harm than good. Certainly healthy upbringing, education, and community values are likelier than taboos to immunize them against violent, degrading, or simple-minded ideas. Censorship may also frustrate young people's developing sense of autonomy and self-respect, and increase their feelings of alienation. Some older children and adolescents are able to process information and make coherent decisions at the same level as many adults. They *need* access to information and ideas precisely because they are in the process of becoming functioning members of society and cannot really do so if they are kept in ideological blinders until they are 18.

These are not simple questions, for they touch not only on our commitment to intellectual freedom but on our society's whole attitude toward educating youth. Feelings that children are raised too permissively, without adequate boundaries on sexual or other behavior, and that adolescents are both directionless and out of control, drive much of the energy that is poured into protectionist censorship campaigns. . . . As the history of childhood shows, none of these adult fears and attitudes is new. But what *are* the best ways to socialize and educate youth—about drugs, violence, racism, and responsible, pleasure-affirming sexuality? Until these questions are confronted, the quick fix of censorship to "protect" the young will continue to have political appeal.

> *"While no system is perfect, effective means of controlling children's access to adult material on the Internet presently exist."*

Children Are Already Protected from Online Pornography

Paul J. Cambria Jr.

Paul J. Cambria Jr. is an attorney for the Adult Freedom Foundation, an organization that works to protect the rights of the adult entertainment industry. In 2006, he took part in a congressional hearing on Internet pornography. In the following viewpoint, excerpted from his testimony before Congress, Cambria argues that further regulations to protect children from online pornography are not necessary. Both Congress and the adult entertainment industry have already enacted sufficient controls, Cambria argues. Further regulations would be both redundant and risk trampling on the First Amendment rights of legitimate pornographers and pornography users.

Paul J. Cambria Jr., "Testimony of Paul J. Cambria, Jr. Esq.," United States Senate Committee on Commerce, Science and Technology, January 19, 2006. Reproduced by permission of the author.

As you read, consider the following questions:

1. How does Cambria define the word *pejorative,* in the context of the viewpoint?
2. According to the author, why is it impossible to write off Internet adult entertainment as mere "pornography?"
3. What is one way named by Cambria that children are already protected from American companies selling adult materials?

During my years of representing the adult entertainment industry, I have come to know first hand the commitment of the industry to providing adults, not children, with legal, mature entertainment. The perspective I have gained through more than a quarter century representing individuals and businesses involved in adult entertainment is unique.... It is my hope that my remarks will bring some balance to a discussion ... that is too often dominated by a vocal minority intent on vilifying expression protected by our Constitution.

My own views concerning adult entertainment and, in particular, its availability on the Internet, are informed by my professional associations, but are tempered by my experiences as a father of five children. With teenagers at home, I share the concerns of parents ... for the welfare of children in all of their activities, including on-line communication. But I also want them to appreciate the true freedom of living under a government that does not succumb to efforts by a motivated minority to restrict the First Amendment rights of the majority of adults by way of speech-limiting schemes camouflaged as child protection or "pornography" initiatives.

A Thriving Business

Indeed, the pejorative phrase "Internet pornography" wrongly marginalizes legitimate adult expression that is accepted by mainstream America in both the marketplace of ideas and the commercial marketplace. Americans spend billions of dollars on adult entertainment each year. Adult Video News, the industry's trade magazine, estimates 2005 industry revenue at approximately $12.6 billion, with over $2.5 billion generated by adult Internet entertainment. The Free Speech Coalition also reports ... that nearly half of the retail outlets in the United States that sell or rent videos also carry adult titles and, in 2002, adult video and DVD rentals and sales at these stores exceeded $3.95 billion. Adult movies are available in approximately forty percent of American hotels, and the nation's major cable and satellite television providers offer many channels of adult programming.

And, of course, adult entertainment is popular among Internet users. A Nielsen/NetRatings study in 2003 estimated that approximately 34 million Americans visited adult entertainment sites on the Internet during August of that year. On an average day, American adult entertainment websites have as many as sixty million unique visitors—far in excess of the unique visitors to even the top news sites in the world. Given its indisputable popularity, Internet adult entertainment cannot be written off as mere "pornography" at the whim of those who refuse to acknowledge that it is an acceptable form of legal entertainment for a substantial segment of our community.

Providing Protection for Children

[Congress] asks whether the government should play a role in controlling so-called "pornography" on the Internet. My answer is that the government already plays a major role, and has at its disposal a variety of powerful tools sufficient to address any concern it may have about adult expression on the Internet—not the least of which is the willingness of the adult entertainment industry to work with Congress to fashion effective solutions to concerns that are proven to be legitimate.

Contrary to the claims of those who wish to stifle any adult expression with an erotic theme, the adult entertainment

Further Testimony: Importance of the Internet

Access by children to age-inappropriate material is a parenting challenge in any medium. Parents must make decisions everyday about the types of content that are appropriate for their children at every stage of their development. While the concerns families harbor about Internet pornography are very real, parents are also realizing that the Internet has become an integral and necessary component of their children's future success in school and, ultimately, in the workplace. The Internet, in all of its myriad manifestations, is not an appliance that parents have the option of simply turning off. Nor should they—even if they were able.

Tim Lordan, testimony before U.S. Senate Committee on Commerce, Science, and Technology, January 19, 2006.

industry does not exploit children. The industry does not employ child performers, and does not condone access by minors to materials created for the entertainment of adults. Put simply, the market for adult entertainment producers is adults, not children. In fact, the adult entertainment industry is a staunch supporter of efforts by the Association of Sites Advocating Child Protection (ASACP), and also supports voluntary labeling and content-rating, and the use of parental filters such as Netnanny.

Laws Already Present

Moreover, adult businesses on the Internet are currently subject to an array of legal requirements. Every American website is governed by the requirements of federal obscenity laws. Similarly, these websites must also comply with strict federal child pornography laws. Consequently, adult entertainment producers were meticulously verifying that their performers were of the age of majority long before federal law in 1995 required them to keep performer identification records.

Additionally, the 2004 CAN-SPAM Act protects children by regulating the marketing by American companies of adult materials through e-mail. Several states have also enacted laws prohibiting the dissemination of harmful materials to minors, and these laws complement long-standing state obscenity and child pornography laws that can also apply to adult entertainment websites.

Consequently, before Congress acts to further burden Internet speech protected by the First Amendment, it should consider the objective need for additional laws, and it should avail itself of the adult entertainment industry's repeatedly rejected offers to assist Congress in fashioning effective and lawful solutions. Congress cannot control through legislation the illegal activities of overseas webmasters or spammers, whose business practices reflect negatively on the Internet as a whole. As seen after the implementation of the CAN-SPAM Act, foreign webmasters will continue to engage in illegal and unethical activities with impunity, resulting in no noticeable impact from the end user's standpoint. It is unjust to punish American webmasters, who are attempting to run ethical and legal businesses, with over-regulation in response to problems caused by those who are beyond the reach of the United States law, and it is equally unfair to exclude the adult entertainment industry from the political process of resolving issues central to the industry.

Working Together

While no system is perfect, effective means of controlling children's access to adult material on the Internet presently exist. For instance, a 2005 study by the Pew Internet and American Life Project revealed that fifty-four percent of Internet-connected families use some sort of filter or monitoring software. Additionally, parents themselves have the means to restrict their children's access to material they deem inappropriate for minors, and implementation of a ".KIDS" domain would assist them in this endeavor.

The adult entertainment industry would also welcome the opportunity to work with Congress and the Department of Justice to explore the potential for age verification systems that employ constitutionally valid standards or a voluntary rating system for adult-oriented content similar to those used by the Motion Picture Association of America, the recording industry, and the video game industry. In the global context of the Internet, the development of effective and affordable voluntary solutions with the help of the adult entertainment industry will certainly have a broader impact than additional laws that burden only American Internet businesses while diminishing their global competitiveness, and stifle in a constitutionally unacceptable manner what is perhaps the world's most valuable source of entertainment and information.

> "I fear that if we do not do more . . .
> then we will lose this fight [against on-
> line pornography] on behalf of our chil-
> dren."

Children Are Not Yet Protected from Online Pornography

Alberto R. Gonzales

Alberto R. Gonzales is the attorney general of the United States under the George W. Bush administration. In the following viewpoint, excerpted from a speech given at the National Center for Missing and Exploited Children, Gonzales argues that the problem of online child pornography is far from resolved. On the contrary, Gonzales states, exploitation of children on the Internet is rampant and growing. Pornographers are finding new and different ways of abusing children and connecting with each other. Further legislation and government initiatives to stop pedophiles and pornographers is essential to ending the problem, he argues.

As you read, consider the following questions:

    1. What are "enticement cases," as defined by the author?

Alberto R. Gonzales, "Prepared Remarks of Attorney General Alberto R. Gonzales," United States Department of Justice, April 20, 2006.

2. What was "Operation Hamlet," as described by Gonzales?

3. What is the new initiative announced by the author?

As you know, there has been a great deal of attention focused on child exploitation issues lately, in the press and by Congress. That is a good thing—the welfare of our children is worthy of debate and examination.

Most of you ..., of course, are painfully aware of how widespread the threat is of pedophiles preying on children online, or abusing kids and sending images of the abuse around the world through the Internet. The threat is frighteningly real, it is growing rapidly, and it must be stopped.

The National Center has done a remarkable job in raising our awareness about the dangers of child sexual abuse, enticement, and pornography. Yet, I think many people still don't appreciate the scope, the nature and the import of this criminal activity, and the threat it poses to our kids.

To educate people about this threat, I am going to describe some of the criminal evidence we have seized. It is graphic, but if we do not talk candidly, then it is easy for people to turn away and worry about other matters. I think it is time to deliver a wake-up call about the true nature and scope of this criminal activity—the depth of the depravity and the harm being inflicted upon innocent children.

Exploitation Not Stopped Yet

I have seen pictures of older men forcing naked young girls to have anal sex. There are videos on the Internet of very young daughters forced to have intercourse and oral sex with their fathers. Viewing this was shocking and it makes my stomach turn. But while these descriptions may make some uncomfortable, we will not defeat this threat unless we all really understand the nature of the child pornography prevalent on the Internet.

As the chief law enforcement officer of the United States, my job is to investigate and prosecute crimes against our children. Changes in technology have made that much more difficult. And of course privacy rights must always be accommodated and protected as we conduct our investigations. But I fear that if we do not do more—if parents, community, business, civic, industry, and political leaders do not work better together, then we will lose this fight on behalf of our children. And so today my message to the American people focuses on two categories of cases: sexual enticement of minors and child pornography.

As you know, enticement cases are those where predators contact kids in chat rooms or through networking sites and arrange to meet in person—with the purpose of making sexual contact.

We've watched as investigative journalists have posed as teens in chat rooms. With great ease, they have lured priests, teachers, doctors, and lawyers, all of whom thought they were going to have sexual contact with children. And we've seen news coverage of high-profile arrests in sting operations.

Of course, the National Center and law enforcement have been focused on identifying, investigating, and prosecuting these offenders for some time. But I welcome the media's recent focus. It's important that the public learns how serious and widespread this threat actually is in America today because of the ease and anonymity of communication over the Internet.

According to one study, one child in every five is solicited online. The television program "Dateline" estimated that, at any given time, 50,000 predators are on the Internet prowling for children. It is simply astonishing how many predators there are, and how aggressively they act.

Educating the public about the enticement threat is especially critical because of the role that parents can play in making sure their children use the Internet safely. It may sound trite, but parents have to be the first line of defense. And I know the National Center works hard to inform parents and kids about online dangers.

Another major type of child exploitation case involves the production, distribution, or possession of child pornography. And this is the area where I am most concerned that people fail to recognize the magnitude of the problem and its impact on children in our society.

Child Pornography Is a Dangerous Crime

To many people, when you mention the term "child pornography," they think of distasteful, but somewhat benign, pictures. Maybe a photograph of a partially nude teenager in a suggestive pose. To them, child pornography is different from the adult pornography that the Supreme Court has said gets First Amendment protection—but only by degree. And they might even add the well-worn notion that child pornography is a victimless crime.

For starters, let's be clear: it is not a victimless crime. Most images today of child pornography depict actual sexual abuse of real children. Each image literally documents a crime scene.

There is nothing mild or benign about child pornography, either. That was true decades ago, when the Supreme Court ruled that child pornography is not entitled to any protection under the First Amendment. And it is certainly true today, where the vast majority of images being produced are far more sinister.

I have already talked about some of the images I have seen at the Child Exploitation and Obscenity Section of the Justice Department. But there are even more shocking and vulgar images we've uncovered. We're talking about a young toddler, tied up with towels, desperately crying in pain while she is being brutally raped and sodomized by an adult man. Another was of a mere infant being savagely penetrated.

In Operation Hamlet, a case principally investigated by the Immigration and Customs Enforcement, we dismantled an international ring of people who were molesting their own children and each other's children. They captured it all on camera, and shared the images. They even did it on web cams sometimes, so that other molesters could watch it live.

These are not just "pornographic" pictures or videos. They are images of graphic sexual and physical abuse of innocent children, even babies. We need to get the public—as well as government officials—to start thinking about it in the right terms. It is brutal, it is heinous, and it is criminal.

A Community of Pedophiles

But understanding the problem goes beyond getting the terminology right. It used to be that child porn was tightly contained by law enforcement, with isolated pornographers relegated to small black markets in underground bookstores or secret mailings. Today, though, pedophiles can download or trade images on the web, through email, in chat rooms or newsgroups, or over peer-to-peer networks or file servers.

Sadly, the Internet age has created a vicious cycle in which child pornography continually becomes more widespread, more graphic, and more sadistic, using younger and younger children. . . . Let me explain a bit, because having the public understand it is critical to appreciating the present state of the problem.

At the most basic level, the Internet is used as a tool for sending and receiving large amounts of child pornography on a relatively anonymous basis. But the Internet has become more than just an expanding supply of images for pedophiles to gratify their urges.

Before the Internet, these pedophiles were isolated—unwelcome even in most adult bookstores. Through the Internet, they have found a community. Offenders can bond with each

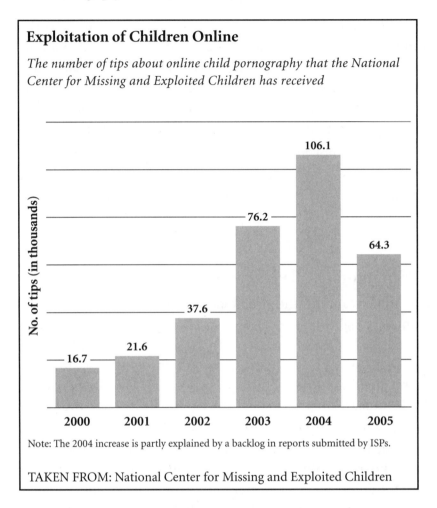

Exploitation of Children Online

The number of tips about online child pornography that the National Center for Missing and Exploited Children has received

No. of tips (in thousands)

- 16.7
- 21.6
- 37.6
- 76.2
- 106.1
- 64.3

2000 2001 2002 2003 2004 2005

Note: The 2004 increase is partly explained by a backlog in reports submitted by ISPs.

TAKEN FROM: National Center for Missing and Exploited Children

other, and the Internet acts as a tool for legitimizing and validating their behavior in their minds. It emboldens them.

And this is where the Internet's vicious cycle leads to the trends I mentioned above. The pedophiles seek to build larger collections of photographs and videos, as a license into their community. As they become de-sensitized to the images they have, they seek more graphic, more heinous, and more disturbing material.

At some point, the pedophiles meet strong incentives not just to collect images, but to produce new ones themselves.

Part of it is the desire to see novel and more graphic images, with younger and younger children. And today's technology makes it easier and less costly for anyone to produce these images and distribute them widely.

The other incentive is that trading rules in parts of this community require that participants offer new pornographic images in order to get images from fellow users. Images of sexual abuse of children become something of a currency—a way to get more pictures. Collectors become producers, and to be in the club, they have to find a child to abuse. And they are driven by the desire for increasingly graphic images.

So the Internet just feeds a vicious cycle. It makes child pornography more accessible and validates the pedophiles' behavior in their minds, driving them to molest even more children and to make new and increasingly vulgar material.

Different Kinds of Child Abuse

The Internet has also fundamentally changed the type of victimization that children endure. Imagine a ten-year-old boy who is sexually abused by a family member. He will always wear the scars of that tragic moment. And stopping the abuse means uprooting the family, which further affects children.

And, because of the Internet and the trends it has caused, he will continue to be victimized in other ways. Pedophiles will often use the images of children as a tool to silence them or to blackmail them into more molestation or pornography—or worse yet, into the horrific trades of child trafficking and prostitution. And the boy will always know that the pictures of his very personal abuse are out there on the Internet, which leads to feelings of embarrassment and helplessness that cause an ongoing and cruel victimization.

Another trend we are seeing is the so-called "molestation on demand," where a pedophile molests a child and others watch live through streaming video. We saw that in the case I mentioned before, Operation Hamlet.

A variation of the on-demand abuse was in *United States v. Mariscal*. We found that Mariscal had been traveling to Cuba and Ecuador over a seven-year period, taking orders from customers to produce child porn to the customers' liking. He would allow customers to write fantasy scripts, and then he would find poverty-stricken families and pay them to allow him to sexually abuse their children, some under the age of 12. And Mariscal would make between $600 and $1,000 per order. To make matters worse, Mariscal was HIV-positive. We caught him and his co-conspirators, and in September 2004 he was sentenced to a 100-year prison term.

I'd like to say that these kinds of criminal behaviors are isolated or rare. Sadly, they are not. It is not an exaggeration to say that we are in the midst of an epidemic in the production and trafficking of movies and images depicting the sexual abuse of children. Now, more than ever, we need to educate the public on the realities of the dangers posed by child sexual predators, abusers, and pornographers.

Ending Exploitation

The question becomes how we, as a society, will respond. There can be only one answer: we cannot, and will not, tolerate those who seek to abuse or exploit our children.

President Bush is absolutely committed to this cause. He has made my mission clear, stating, and I quote, "Anyone who targets a child for harm will be a primary target of law enforcement."

At the Department [of Justice], we are working more of these cases than ever before in the Child Exploitation and Obscenity Section, in the FBI's Innocent Images Unit, and in U.S. Attorneys' Offices around the country. We are funding the Internet Crimes Against Children program [ICAC], a successful network of 45 task forces that I know you all work with closely. Under President Bush the funding for the ICAC program has more than doubled, to over $14 million in fiscal year 2006.

On February 15th [2006]—following the President's directive to protect our children—I announced Project Safe Childhood, an initiative aimed at combating the online exploitation and victimization of children.

Through Project Safe Childhood, we will build on our efforts in this area by making law enforcement at all levels more coordinated, better trained, and more involved. And we will use our federal resources at the Justice Department to make sure we find these criminals and keep them away from our kids.

We are moving closer to formally implementing Project Safe Childhood, after soliciting support and suggestions from a number of people and organizations, including the National Center. . . . It is my hope that this new program will make a real difference in the lives of Americans, and especially our children.

But in order for Project Safe Childhood to succeed, we have to make sure law enforcement has all the tools and information it needs to wage this battle. The investigation and prosecution of child predators depends critically on the availability of evidence that is often in the hands of Internet service providers. This evidence will be available for us to use only if the providers retain the records for a reasonable amount of time. Unfortunately, the failure of some Internet service providers to keep records has hampered our ability to conduct investigations in this area.

As a result, I have asked the appropriate experts at the Department to examine this issue and provide me with proposed recommendations. And I will reach out personally to the CEOs [chief executive officers] of the leading service providers, and to other industry leaders, to solicit their input and assistance. Record retention by Internet service providers consistent with the legitimate privacy rights of Americans is an issue that must be addressed.

I am also proud to announce . . . that the Administration will send to Congress a new piece of legislation, the Child Pornography and Obscenity Prevention Amendments of 2006. This legislation will help ensure that communications providers report the presence of child pornography on their systems by strengthening criminal penalties for failing to report it. It will also prevent people from inadvertently stumbling across pornographic images on the Internet. . . .

I have directed my staff to see what else we can do. But all our efforts, including Project Safe Childhood is built with the recognition that law enforcement cannot do it alone. It has to be a community effort, down to every last parent.

Help from Organizations

I can't overstate how important the National Center will be to making Project Safe Childhood a success. . . .

Before announcing Project Safe Childhood, I spoke with [National Center] director, Ernie Allen, and asked for his help. I was very pleased that he immediately embraced the initiative wholeheartedly, and I look forward to continuing to work together as full partners.

One of the most critical parts of implementing Project Safe Childhood will be to provide the right training to investigators and prosecutors around the country. As I've discussed today, they need to better understand the scope and nature of this criminal activity, and they need to know how to work computer-based investigations and prosecutions, and how to work cooperatively on leads.

The National Center is experienced in facilitating that kind of training, and Ernie has committed to providing training in the critical early stages of the initiative. And we'll also work with our other partners . . . that provide ongoing training programs. . . .

The National Center helps in so many other ways, too. The CyberTipline . . . plays an essential role for law enforcement, centralizing the place for people to report crimes against children. [The National Center is] also on the cutting edge of efforts to identify and rescue the kids we see being abused in pornographic images, through [its] Exploited Child Unit and the National Child Victim Identification Program. Project Safe Childhood will help bring together [the Center's] critical efforts and the federal, state, and local law enforcement of officials working in each district around the Nation.

With [the Center's] help, law enforcement is working to stem the surge in child exploitation and pornography. But the scope of the problem is immense. I am therefore calling on all responsible Americans and corporate citizens—down to every last parent, teacher, and minister—to educate themselves about the problem and see how they can help out. Together, we can make our homes and our neighborhoods safer for our sons and daughters.

| *"The worst kind of legal and illegal filth is still readily available on library computers."*

Libraries Should Put Filtering Software on Their Computers

Don S. Otis

In the following viewpoint from the conservative Christian organization the American Family Association, Don S. Otis argues that children must be protected from pornography in public libraries. The American Library Association's refusal to install filtering software on their computers is dangerous, Otis argues, and is harming children's innocence in the name of the First Amendment. Though children do have rights, these rights should not take precedent over morality. Don S. Otis has written two books on morality and children.

As you read, consider the following questions:

1. According to the author, what is the purpose of libraries?

2. What percentage of teens stated that they had visited pornographic Web sites, according to a study cited by Otis?

3. What is the definition of "emasculation," as given by the author?

I remember my first experience with pornography. I was 8, maybe 9 years old at the time.

My slightly older brother had convinced me to take his paper route for the day. What I remember most was not throwing papers on the sprawling lawns of a middle-class neighborhood—instead, it was the glossy image in the center of a pornographic magazine that I came across at an old abandoned gas station in a Southern California suburb. Now, nearly four decades later, I still remember exactly what I saw that day.

So, when my two sons came home from the East Bonner County Public Library one day, I was appalled at what they told me. "Dad," my 14-year-old said, "did you know kids are looking at pornography on the computers at the library?"

My first response was, it can't be true. Libraries are supposed to be places where children learn, where they are protected, where responsible adults offer reasonable guidance. I moved from Los Angeles to Sandpoint, Idaho, to raise my kids in a more wholesome environment. This is one of the most conservative states in the nation. Pornography on the library computers—could I be that naive?

I did some investigating.

Looking at Pornography in Libraries

I read library policy, asked questions, read the American Library Association (ALA) handbooks and policies. Sure enough, our brand-new public library was now the only X-rated shop in town. Our beautiful taxpayer-funded facility is situated right between an elementary school, middle school and high school. Children flock to the library after school—often surfing the Internet for pornography.

American Library Association Policy

Librarians nationwide today are working in a changed environment. We continue to oppose the use of filters that block access to constitutionally protected speech and believe filters are not the best way to ensure library users have a safe and enriching online experience. . . .

Equity of access is a core value of the library profession and the ALA, and we must be clear that installing filters that block access to safe and legal information deepens the digital divide between those who have Internet access at home, work or school and those who 'have not.' Public libraries are the main access point for millions of Americans who do not otherwise have access to the wide world of information available online, and we must ensure that libraries continue to serve all people equally.

Carla Hayden, American Library Association, 2003.

More than 50% of teens revealed they have visited websites containing pornography in a study by the National Coalition for the Protection of Children & Families; 79% of them have done so on a library or school computer.

The more I learned about the lack of protection for children in my own community, the less naive and the more vigilant I became. In my own small town of 6,000, the library director, chairman and the entire board of trustees have surrendered to the agenda of the ALA.

In an interview on a local talk show, the library director boldly quizzed his interviewer with the following question: "I am asking you, is there a danger in viewing pornography? What would that danger be?" This statement became the catalyst for my own involvement in a grassroots, community-wide, interdenominational effort called Bonner County Citizens for Sound Library Policies.

We canvassed the community, collecting more than 1,600 signatures from concerned parents, businesspeople and teachers. The pressure forced a halfhearted solution by library trustees—to provide a handful of computer systems that will be filtered for minors (but only with the written requirement from each child's parent).

This is clearly not enough. The worst kind of legal and illegal filth is still readily available on library computers (leaving us no choice but to vote reasonable people on to the board).

Trustees and library directors nationwide cower behind so-called First Amendment rights—a mantra for the religion of humanism. With nearly 9,000 public libraries scattered across the United States, Internet pornography—not to mention hate sites—now pose a serious danger to children and families.

Children Must Be Protected

With the passage of the Children's Internet Protection Act (CIPA), schools and libraries that do not provide filtered access for minors will lose e-rate subsidies. So far, only 21% provide protective filtering, according to a *School Library Journal* article in January [2001]. It is no surprise that the ALA and the American Civil Liberties Union are challenging the act because they believe it violates First Amendment protections; the ACLU, in fact, remains one of the few ardent supporters for legalizing child pornography. According to the ACLU Report on Filtering in Libraries, "Students do have First Amendment rights, and blocking software is inappropriate, especially for junior [high] and high school students."

Today we face the emasculation [loss of power] of moral sanity under the guise of freedom of speech. It doesn't seem to matter whether children are protected from pornographers, pedophiles or rapists—our so-called freedoms must prevail at all costs. Never mind that librarians have a long history of selecting what materials they will place on their shelves and which they will not. Any librarian who dares to stand for reasonable standards risks the intolerance of the ALA.

Your children and mine are at risk like never before. An Internet savvy adult or child can type in key words and find pornography spilling out of every pixel of their four-color screen.

I am weary of hearing how filtering software doesn't work or that it blocks educational sites. This argument is simply a smokescreen. Filtering software works—and it is getting more sophisticated all the time. Without filtering software, anyone can type in a keyword to study the White House and find a porn site. Or, more insidious, type in Disney, Britney Spears, Pokemon, toys or candy and gain access to porn sites.

Why, I wonder, are pornographers targeting our children? And why are libraries so intent to protect the very material that degrades women, ruins families and encourages rapists and pedophiles? At least one answer is that pornographers know if they can hook boys at a young age the addictive effects will last a lifetime.

No wonder Jesus said, "And if anyone causes one of these little ones who believe in me to sin, it would be better for him to be thrown into the sea with a large millstone tied around his neck" (Mark 9:42).

Steal a child's innocence and you shatter his faith. As [eighteenth-century British philosopher] Sir Edmund Burke wisely observed, "Tell me what are the prevailing sentiments that occupy the minds of your young people and I will tell you what is to be the character of the next generation." A morally prudent society can ill afford to ignore the senseless arguments espoused by those intolerant of Judeo-Christian principles.

> "We are not going to protect our kids
> from sexually explicit material by pass-
> ing laws and installing electronic de-
> vices on our computers."

Libraries Should Not Put Filtering Software on Their Computers

Hank Nichols

In the following viewpoint, Hank Nichols argues that installing pornography filters on computers in public libraries limits freedom of information. Congress has approved filters because they filter out "obscene" material, Nichols writes, which might harm children. But the definition of "obscene" is malleable and subject to opinion. Material once thought obscene is now socially acceptable. In addition, Nichols argues, the best way to protect children from pornography is to educate them at home, rather than forcing librarians to be censors.

As you read, consider the following questions:

1. What does the Children's Internet Protection Act require schools and libraries to do, according to Nichols?

Hank Nichols, "Forced Library Filtering Is Censorship," *Boston Globe*, January 27, 2002, p. 14. Reproduced by permission of the author.

2. As cited by the author, how does the Hicklin rule define "obscenity"?

3. How did the librarians at the workshop Nichols attended feel about computer filters?

I've seen a possible future, and I didn't like it very much.

My peek into what may lie ahead came at a workshop on intellectual freedom, sponsored by the New Hampshire Library Trustees Association. The focus of the workshop was the Children's Internet Protection Act, which was signed into law by [former] President Bill Clinton on Dec. 22, 2000.

This federal law requires schools and libraries that receive federal funds for Internet access to install filtering software that will keep our kids from checking out porno sites while at the local town or school library. The discussion ranged from the technical (the filters don't work well) to the constitutional (What about the First Amendment?).

Just the mention of the topic took me back to my 16th birthday. Getting a driver's license was at the top of my list that year, but I was nonetheless intrigued by the present one of my sisters gave me. She was an English major at the University of New Hampshire, and my gift from her that year was a book that came in a plain brown wrapper. It was an obscene book, one that could not be printed, sold, or distributed in the United States.

When the time was right I retreated to my room, closed the door behind me, and opened my present with great anticipation. An obscene book of my very own! The book was "Lady Chatterley's Lover" by D. H. Lawrence. I was more puzzled than disappointed. I'm not sure I ever found the naughty parts.

"Lady Chatterley" was obscene because of the way we defined obscenity. Our courts relied on the Hicklin rule, a definition of obscenity borrowed from British courts in the 1820s.

CIPA and Censorship

The Children's Internet Protection Act [CIPA] clearly violates the constitutional right to freedom of speech. Libraries have been designated by the government as places where speech may be freely received and freely expressed. Accordingly, the government may not restrict the right of citizens to access speech that is legally protected, and that is what CIPA does. There is not agreement in our society about limitations that may be imposed on sexually explicit speech. In the case of CIPA, the bottom line comes down to balancing this question: is it better to block protected speech in the course of blocking unprotected speech? Congress is in favor of this action, while information professionals and civil liberties experts strongly oppose it.

Lynn Sutton, MLA Forum, February 20, 2002.

The Hicklin rule said something was obscene ". . . if it tends to deprave and corrupt those whose minds are open to such immoral influences and into whose hands it may happen to fall."

Loosely translated, the Hicklin rule said if it's not suitable for children, it's not suitable for anyone. And if any part of the work is obscene, the whole work is obscene. There go[es] "Lady Chatterley's Lover," "Ulysses," and an endless list of books and other works of art that might, just might, not be appropriate for children.

The Definition of Obscenity

In the 1950s, public pressure forced the Supreme Court to come up with a definition of obscenity that would permit adults to enjoy material suitable for adults. Since then, the definition of obscenity has changed, but one thing has not.

No matter how you define it, the nation's highest court said, obscenity is not protected by the First Amendment.

[In the twenty-first century] you don't have to look long or far to see how much things have changed since the Hicklin rule was dropped. Were I to go into an adult bookstore today and ask for "Lady Chatterley's Lover," I'd be greeted with quizzical looks or I'd be laughed out of the store. The sexually explicit material we see around is pornographic, which means it is legal, stuff that doesn't go "too far," wherever that is.

Which brings us back to our libraries, schools, and the Internet. The Internet Children's Protection Act and the kind of thinking that goes with it can take us back to the Hicklin rule in a flash. Suddenly, in our libraries, we may be confronted with a situation where we only have access to material suitable for children.

Filters are an interesting concept and if parents want to put filters on their computers at home, I guess that's their business. But all the reports I've read indicate that the filters don't work well. They can deny you access to some legitimate information because of the wording. Forget looking up a recipe for breast of chicken. And sometimes crafty Web site designers can come up with porno sites that slip by the filters as deftly as a cat slipping through a hole that seems half its size.

When one library installed filters on its computers recently, young folks took an increased interest in working at the computers for a few days. Then interest dropped off again. The kids had found a way to hack through the filters.

Librarians Are Not Censors

We are not going to protect our kids from sexually explicit material by passing laws and installing electronic devices on our computers and television sets. It is more than just not fair to ask our schools and libraries to put filters on their computers. Asking our librarians to become censors is contrary to the

principles of intellectual freedom upon which our libraries are based. Our libraries are not just homes to those works with which we all agree. They are sanctuaries where the free exchange of ideas can occur undisturbed. The librarians at the workshop I attended were united in their opposition to filters and other forms of censorship. We are starting down a dangerous road if we ask our librarians to become arbiters of what's appropriate.

Internet porno is a problem we will have to deal with in our homes and in our classrooms, not in Congress or in our courts. A good antidote to pornography is competent sex education that exposes pornography for the fantasy money machine that it really is. I never had much luck with sex education and my two sons. Every time I brought up the topic they clamped their hands over their ears and hummed loudly, making sure that not one syllable got through. I've always been grateful for the sex education they received at school.

At home and in our libraries we need to work together to encourage the responsible use of computers. Many schools and libraries now have agreements for parents to sign, regarding how these public computers will and will not be used by their children. That's censorship enough.

We can't protect our kids from exposure to pornography. The best we can hope for is to educate them in a way that allows them to grow up with a healthy attitude toward sex and an understanding of the pathetic porno they will encounter on the Internet and, eventually, among adult video and book merchants.

"Federal obscenity laws are the only legal weapon available against Internet pornography."

Legislation Is the Best Way to Protect Children on Social Networking Sites

Tom Rodgers

In the following viewpoint, Tom Rodgers takes a firm antipornography stance, arguing that social-networking sites such as Myspace.com should be controlled. Pornography is readily available to children and teenagers on this site, and it is unquestionably harmful for them to view, Rodgers contends. Internet obscenity laws should include social-networking sites, he argues, and must be enforced. Rodgers is a retired police officer and consultant for Morality in Media, a conservative antipornography organization.

As you read, consider the following questions:

1. How many complaints about Myspace.com had Morality in Media received from May 2, 2004, to September 2006, according to Rodgers?

2. What percentage of the online social networking traffic does Myspace.com control, according to a *USA Today* article cited by the author?

3. Which Supreme Court case does Rodgers say decided that the First Amendment does not protect obscene materials?

In its "To Catch a Predator" series, NBC TV's *Dateline* teamed up with an Internet watchdog organization called Perverted Justice to fight against Internet sex predators. Early episodes of the series showcased the popular website MySpace.com, showing how pedophiles are using this site to shop for children on the Internet for sexual purposes. In these episodes, Perverted Justice investigators, working in conjunction with law enforcement, pose as decoys and make contacts through Myspace.com. As a result, dozens of men have been arrested for a variety of charges.

What is equally disturbing is the large number of on-line obscenity complaints about Myspace.com that have been received at Morality in Media's (MIM) www.obscenitycrimes.org web site. Unlike the *Dateline* series, the MIM complaints are not about sexual predators stalking children online, but about the pornography that is readily available on or through Myspace.

MIM has two consultants who validate these complaints. Both consultants are retired law enforcement agents with experience in investigating obscenity crimes. Once these complaints have been validated, the consultants then write and submit detailed reports to the Justice Department for investigation, follow-up and potential prosecution.

MySpace.com is a site where people can find other people with similar interests and post information on blogs regarding a variety of subjects. It is sort of a cyber social club. People can go there for free and research information on all kinds of ordinary subjects like films, music, forums, comedy, classi-

File-Sharing Artworks: Another Area of Concern

It's happening right under parents' noses, yet few know that their teens and young children are being targeted in a new battle-tactic of the pornography industry. Peer-to-peer file-sharing programs represent a widely popular new trend among today's youth.

In the 1990s, Napster was forced to shut down to protect copyrighted music, and recently the Recording Industry Association of America (RIAA) announced plans to sue users trading music files. However, the new "peer-to-peer," or P2P, networks—such as Kazaa, Morpheus, and Grokster—pose a new and far greater problem than the illegal trade of music. These P2P networks allow children to easily download videos and images of free pornography and illegal child pornography, and also create a new arena for pedophiles.

Kathryn Hooks, National Review, *July 22, 2003.*

fieds, and more. They can also view pornographic pictures and videos, and children are only a few clicks away from being exposed to pornography at MySpace.

Free Pornography Available

[From] May 2, 2004, [to September 2006,] MIM received approximately one hundred and sixty complaints from citizens about MySpace.com. This includes complaints where children have been exposed to unwanted "porn spam" or to pornography while searching for other content and complaints where children have knowingly exhibited pornography on their own web sites.

In an email to MIM, one concerned parent asked, "I would like to know how a website such as myspace.com is able to have pornographic material available through its users if the site was designed for children 14 and over.... Some children under the age of 18 have soft to hardcore porn within their pages, often pictures of themselves. Myspace.com appears to be nothing but a great opportunity for children to have complete access to porn. I would like to know if and what the regulations for this site are (sic)."

Curious onlookers were also subjected to unwanted graphic sexual acts and printed information. One complainant stated, "A large number of underage users are posting and reading obscenity and pictures." A second complainant commented, "16 year old girls allowed to discuss bestiality." A third stated that he/she had received uninvited pornography through an instant message from some unknown person signed on through Myspace. Many Myspace web pages also have direct links to commercial pornographic web sites that offer free "teasers" (pornographic photos or videos that can be viewed without proof of age), in addition to full subscriptions that require payment. Upon checking a recent complaint on Myspace.com, one of the MIM consultants reported that a pornographic video automatically began playing as soon as the Myspace page was opened up.

It would be very difficult to find a young teen that has never heard of Myspace.com. In fact, it is surprising how many teens have actually set up their own MySpace blogs. It is the vogue thing to do. As a teenager, if you do not have your own blog then you have not kept up with the changes. It is shocking to see all the personal and potentially damaging information that people, including teens, are posting about themselves and their families on these sites.

[While it] may seem like an innocent blog site and fun place for teens, Myspace.com can, ... be a very dangerous place for children to spend time. So what are the chances of your children visiting Myspace.com? The number of visitors is steadily increasing, as Myspace.com went from 4.9 million

U.S. visitors in 2004, to more than 50 million U.S. visitors in May 2006. According to a [August 2006] article in *USA Today*, MySpace had 95 million members and more than 81% of the online social networking traffic.

Enforce Obscenity Laws

Pornography is invading just about every aspect of our lives. It has come into our communities with so-called "adult businesses" and into the so-called family video stores that contain the "adult sections." It has invaded our schools, libraries, churches and job sites via the Internet. Because pornography might seem to be everywhere, there are a lot of people who believe that pornography is okay, acceptable, and perhaps even legal. But, as Roger Young, a retired FBI Agent and MIM Consultant, teaches, "Americans have been misled, misinformed, and wrongly educated that pornography is okay, acceptable and perhaps even legal, when it is not!"

In the 1973 *Miller v. California* case, the Supreme Court held that the First Amendment does not protect obscene materials and that obscenity laws can be enforced against hardcore pornography. In 1996, Congress updated federal obscenity laws to clarify that distribution of obscenity on the Internet is a crime; and at this point federal obscenity laws are the only legal weapon available against Internet pornography because the Child Online Protection Act, which is intended to restrict children's access to Internet porn, is still tied up in the courts. [The Supreme Court ruled the act unconstitutional in late 2006.]

Most people do not want the Internet to become a cesspool of hardcore pornography. They do not want children being exposed to hardcore pornography. My question is this: When will Americans (parents in particular) get fed up with the flood of Internet pornography pouring into their communities and homes and insist that Internet obscenity laws be enforced?

> *"Educate yourself and your child on the risks that exist online. That way you can reap the benefits of the Internet while skirting the dangers."*

Education Is the Best Way to Protect Children on Social Networking Sites

Alan Cohen

Alan Cohen is a freelance writer and contributor to PC Magazine, *from which this viewpoint is excerpted. Cohen writes that the best way to keep children from predators and pornography on social networking sites such as Myspace.com is to educate them on how to handle potentially dangerous situations. Preventing children from using these sites will only increase their allure, Cohen contends, and the sites cannot be trusted to effectively police themselves. Filters are only somewhat effective. Teaching children how to protect themselves online is the best way to keep them safe, he maintains.*

As you read, consider the following questions:

1. What is one particular challenge for parents in monitoring their children's Internet use, according to Cohen?

2. What percent of parents allow their children to use a computer in a private area of their home, according to the author?

3. In Cohen's opinion, why is filtering software only somewhat effective?

Every few weeks, David Frey walks into a school cafeteria, pops open his laptop, and frightens a room full of parents. There's nothing particularly scary about Frey himself, a friendly 39-year-old with a wry sense of humor. It's all in his presentation.

An assistant district attorney of Staten Island, New York, and chief of his office's computer and technology investigations unit, Frey has seen practically every bad act that can happen via the Internet, from drug deals set up in AOL chat rooms to sexual predators targeting—and assaulting—minors. Almost without exception, the parents [he] speaks to have noticed nothing to be wary of. "Most parents are completely surprised when I show them this stuff," says Frey. "They have no idea what goes on online."

Although many parents are in the dark about their kids' online activities, there's nothing secret in Frey's laptop. And that, says Frey, is an even bigger problem. With social networking sites such as MySpace.com, Facebook, and Xanga exploding in popularity, teenage diaries are no longer hidden under the bed. They're posted online, often freely accessible to anyone, anywhere. Bits of information that seem perfectly innocuous—a first name, a school name, interests, and worries—can be seen and used by sexual predators, for whom the Internet has become, Frey says, "a target-rich environment."

Before visiting a school Frey will search for, and easily find, MySpace pages belonging to students at that school. These are what he shows the parents, and these are what shock them. "Here's one," says Frey, shaking his head as he pulls up a teenage girl's MySpace page in his conference room. "For a pedophile, this page is just perfect."

At first glance, there doesn't seem to be anything extraordinary about the page. A young girl writes about her struggle with bulimia, her drug use, and her lack of self-esteem. It's troubling stuff, to be sure, but no different from hundreds of other pages Frey has accessed on the Internet. That, too, says Frey, is the problem: "Kids don't think of the Internet as something everyone sees. They are completely trusting. They say things they'd never tell their parents." The irony is that although their parents may not know about any of this, online predators, who tend to target the most vulnerable kids, now do.

"Look at this," says Frey, pointing to the screen. "She posts her photo and gives her name. Then she posts the name of her high school, her e-mail address, her AOL Instant Messenger name, and all of her interests—the singers and movies she likes."

For a predator this is both a dossier and an opportunity. "If I'm a pedophile, I now know that she has a bad self-image, I know where she goes to school, I know the things she likes," says Frey. "I know that she's in drama class. She even says where she works." All of this, he says, creates easy pickings for a predator, who will know how to make contact with the teen and how to gain her trust. It's simple to say all the right things when you're practically handed an instruction manual.

"Predators are very clever," says Frey. "They use the data you've posted to pretend to be a friend. They groom you; they get your trust. It's not sexual at first. But gradually they push a little bit, then they fall back, then they push—until it's completely sexual." Often predators will send pornography to the kids they are targeting to desensitize them to sexual activity, explaining that it's no big deal and that everybody does it. Then comes the final push: a suggestion to meet. "This girl," says Frey, looking at the profile on his laptop and shaking his head once more, "is the perfect victim."

Kids at Risk

The Internet may have broadened our view of the world and made our professional lives easier, but it has certainly complicated parenting. Of course, the problem is not exactly new. Even before social-networking sites came on the scene, parents had good reason to worry about their kids' safety online.

Frey started giving his talks—to parents, kids, guidance counselors, and other prosecutors—in 2000, the same year that a study by the National Center for Missing & Exploited Children found that one in five children who use the Internet had been sexually solicited online.

Back in 2000 the main targets of concern were chat rooms and instant messaging. Now there are blogs and social-networking sites to worry about. For both parents and kids, these new technologies can be even more problematic. "In a chat room, a predator goes in cold," says Frey. "On these new sites, predators know about you, they know about your friends, they have all of this data about you." And they know how to use it.

The burgeoning popularity of social networking sites—MySpace has over 75 million users—means that even preteens are clamoring to use them. Although MySpace warns users that they must be 14 or older to register, the site has no way of verifying age. The same is true for almost all other social networking sites. "We know that younger children are lying to get on the sites," says Nancy McBride, the national safety director at the National Center for Missing & Exploited Children.

Making matters worse: Online predators aren't the only danger parents have to fear. The ubiquity of broadband now makes it easier for kids to be exposed to pornography and other objectionable video and images. Cyberbullying, where kids are threatened via anonymous e-mail, instant messages, and even full-blown Web sites, is an increasingly common and worrisome problem.

Then there's all the personal information kids post online. Not only does it expose them to predators, it puts them at risk for identity theft. And even if there are no criminals reading your MySpace page, well, maybe there is a college admissions officer taking a look. "Kids think they're talking to other kids, but they have no idea who they are speaking to," says McBride. "They'll post pictures of illegal or inappropriate behavior and it will come back to haunt them when they apply to schools or for a job."

Advice to Parents: Learn This Stuff

Keeping all of these perils in check can be a full-time job for a parent, and it's a job they're not doing so well. One particular challenge is that most kids know a lot more about the Internet than do their parents, and they use the knowledge gap to win more time and less supervision online. "You find that a lot of parents are bullied," says Frey. "They don't want to look stupid in front of their kids, who tell them that everyone is doing it."

Bridging that knowledge gap is essential to understanding the risks your children face online and how you can help them. "If you're a parent, you better learn about this stuff," says McBride. "If that means taking a class, or getting a book, so be it. It's hard to protect your kids online if you don't know what they're doing." Once parents understand the technologies and the dangers, they can more easily talk to their kids about those dangers and how to avoid them.

Sadly, this common-sense solution—educating both yourself and your children about staying safe online—is in reality often neglected. Even though it's hard to read the daily newspaper nowadays without coming upon a story about an online predator or some cyberstalking or cyberbullying incident, 30 percent of parents allow their teenage children to use a computer in a private area of their home, according to a 2005 sur-

Interaction Education

Nobody's denying there are predators online. But banning social networks in schools and libraries is only likely to make the problem worse.

Why? Because it means we're abdicating our responsibility to teach children about how to interact online. And believe me, in the process of teaching children how to interact online, we could all learn a thing or two ourselves.

Stephen Bryant, Publish, May 11, 2006.

vey by Cox Communications and the National Center for Missing & Exploited Children.

That's exactly the wrong thing to do, say online-safety experts, who urge parents to take the computer out of the bedroom and put it in a common area, like a family room or den, where children have no expectation of privacy and parents can check on what they're doing. Just a little bit of education, the experts say, and parents would quickly understand how necessary this rule of thumb is.

Filters: A False Sense of Security

If that little bit of education isn't getting through, the fault doesn't lie completely with parents. Criminal penalties, technological solutions such as filtering software that blocks inappropriate sites, and pressure on content providers to police their own sites are getting the bulk of media—and political— coverage. Not surprisingly, many parents have been lulled into believing that these approaches will take care of the problem—wishful, and dangerous, thinking.

"What parents have to realize is that there is no silver bullet," says Herbert Lin, senior scientist at the National Research Council of the National Academies, where he directed a 2002 study on protecting children from sexual exploitation and online pornography. "Filtering software has certainly gotten better, but do parents rely on it too much? In my opinion, they do. A filter is brittle. Even if it stops 90 percent of the bad stuff, what do you do about the other 10 percent? You still have to have a thorough educational process."

[In 2002], Lin emphasized the need for education in online safety in his report, and he's still waiting for legislators to pick up on the idea. "We said education was fundamental, but no one is taking that seriously," says Lin. "It's not sexy; it's not easy to do. You don't see any bills on education." The focus, instead, has been on criminal penalties and filtering software. These, say Lin, should be part of the answer, but not the answer itself: "Any solution that says you don't have to do the hard work of being a parent is not going to work."

Nor should parents rely on content providers to find predators and porn. To be sure, the sites are ramping up their own enforcement efforts. Both MySpace and Facebook recently hired chief privacy officers. MySpace runs public service ads to promote online safety and reviews all images on its site. Facebook warns users who may be abusing the system. "We'll look for things like the number of rejected friend requests they have," says Chris Kelly, Facebook's chief privacy officer.

But with social networking sites growing so rapidly, inappropriate content and behavior is bound to slip through the nets. MySpace may be reviewing images, but it receives two million of them each day, and keeping an eye on all of them is a tall order.

Parents need to understand what can and does happen online, but just as important is their need to develop a line of communication with their children. This is crucial not only to prevent harm, but also to take action should inappropriate activity take place.

The good news is that even as the technologies get more sophisticated, so too have police and prosecutors. "Law enforcement is much better trained about this now," says

McBride of the National Center for Missing & Exploited Children. Internet investigation units are also better staffed and funded. The Department of Justice finances 45 Internet Crimes Against Children task forces, and many local police departments now have units dedicated to investigating Internet crimes. Even cyberbullies hiding behind anonymous e-mail accounts, proxy servers, or a neighbor's WiFi network can usually be tracked down quickly.

"They may be clever, but we're more clever." says Frey. "A lot of times they'll leak a tell [an identifying item]. They'll target people they know; they'll use their pet's name, or their ZIP code, or their school in their screen name. You look for a guy with a pit bull named Randy. It isn't hard. We'll get 90 to 95 percent of the people we're looking for if it's reported."

And there's the rub. The best detective work in the world is of little use if kids and parents don't report inappropriate activity in a timely fashion. ISPs [Internet service providers] usually can't trace activity back to a specific user after a certain time period. "If we send a letter asking them to preserve data, they'll preserve it," says Frey. "The problem is when someone doesn't make a report in time, and we lose the path."

House Rules

Though Frey's presentation is intended to scare parents, he doesn't want to scare them too badly. Then they might pull the plug on the Internet altogether, and that, he and other experts say, probably does more harm than good: It deprives children of a remarkable resource and can breed defiance. "Kids are always going to find a way to use it," says McBride.

The better strategy is to give kids access—but set some rules. Keep the PC in a place where there is little privacy, and visit sites with your child when possible. Let your kids know that it's important to tell you if they are ever approached online or receive inappropriate content. Don't delete any messages or images, either; they can help law enforcement trace the activity back to its source.

Teach your kids the "embarrassment rule": They should never post anything they wouldn't want the whole world to read, because once they post it, the whole world can read it. Tell them to be careful about what they post about friends, too. Some of the most predator-friendly information (names, telephone numbers, employers) isn't left by the author of a MySpace page, but by friends posting comments.

Recognize the Red Flags

Keep in mind, too, that while preventive steps like these can reduce the risks, they can't eliminate them completely. So watch for red flags. Is your child minimizing or changing a browser window whenever you walk into the room? Is he using instant message lingo like "POS" (parent over shoulder)? Is he getting phone calls from people you don't know or wearing new clothes? They could be gifts from a predator. Is your child reluctant to log on or go to school? Those could be signs he's being cyberbullied. And if you think there is a problem, report it.

The National Center for Missing & Exploited Children runs a hotline, both on the Web at www.cybertipline.com and via telephone at 800-843-5678. Someone will review your report and forward it to the proper authorities. Let your Internet service provider know, too. ISPs face fines for failing to report child pornography on their systems—fines that the Bush Administration is seeking to raise under the proposed Child Pornography and Obscenity Prevention Amendments of 2006.

Most important of all, you want to educate yourself and your child on the risks that exist online. That way you can reap the benefits of the Internet while skirting the dangers.

"The Internet is a great thing but it's also dangerous—like a swimming pool," says Lin. "Do you want to have fences? Sure. Do you want to have locks? You do. Do you want to have laws that make people liable? Yes. But the safest kid is the kid who knows how to swim."

If you're a parent, you'd better learn about this stuff. If that means taking a class or getting a book, so be it. It's hard to protect your kids online if you don't know what they're doing.

A Predator's Path

An online predator can turn a little info into a lot of trouble.

Amanda's MySpace page looks innocuous enough: She posted her first name, her school and interests. She writes a lot about how her parents and teachers just don't understand her.

A predator draws a conclusion: Amanda just might be on the high school's softball team. He Googles the high school, finds a photo of the team—and recognizes her. He now has Amanda's last name.

The predator heads back to Google: He enters her full name and her school name, and finds a local newspaper story about a fund-raiser Amanda's father spearheaded for new equipment for the softball team.

A new Web search: Google provides the predator with the addresses of all the Alfred Simpsons in the city. Only one of the dozen listings is near Amanda's school. The predator now knows where Amanda lives.

From here, the predator is home free: He knows where to find her. Striking up a conversation—say, on a softball field—won't be a problem. Neither will be gaining her trust. He can say all the right things—like how his parents never understood him, either.

In a short time, the predator has contacted Amanda: The e-mails and IMs are harmless enough, and Amanda's new friend is always so friendly and reassuring. Finally, Amanda thinks, there is an adult who understands her.

The messages are getting a bit explicit: Amanda says so, and the predator tones things down. He sends her a new softball glove, too. When the messages get sexual again, she figures he's right, everyone does talk about—and do—this stuff. So when he suggests they meet up, she thinks: Why not?

10 Essential Tips for Parents

Here's some practical advice for keeping your kids safe online:

1. Don't forbid Internet use; in all probability, your kids will defy your ban on the sly.

2. Filtering software won't block all dangers your kids face on the Web, but it's a good start. Also visit sites with your child whenever possible.

3. Understand the technologies: Take a class . . . try the sites yourself. The more you know about the Internet, the better you can talk to your kids about it.

4. Place the computer in a common area of your home; kids won't expect privacy there.

5. Talk to the parents of your child's friends; most kids use computers at friends' homes.

6. Teach your kids the "embarrassment rule": They should never post anything they wouldn't want everyone to read.

7. Tell them to be careful about what they post regarding other people. Predator-friendly information is often left by friends posting comments.

8. Let your child know that it's important to tell you if he or she is ever approached online or receives inappropriate content.

9. Look for red flags that your child is in danger, such as minimizing a browser when you enter the room and getting phone calls from people you don't know.

10. If you think there may be a problem, report it to authorities and also to your Internet service provider.

Periodical Bibliography

The following articles have been selected to supplement the diverse view presented in this chapter.

Arthur Bowker	"The Cybersex Offender and Children," *FBI Law Enforcement Bulletin*, March 2005.
BusinessWeek Online	"Making MySpace Safe for Kids," March 6, 2006.
Lance Dickie	"The Best Information Filter Is Your Local Librarian," *Seattle Times*, July 4, 2003.
Economist	"Buried by a Pile of Porn," January 18, 2003.
Cori Howard	"Internet Vigilante," *Maclean's*, June 6, 2005.
Jeffery Kosseff	"Bill Proposes Library Porn Filters," *Portland Oregonian*, February 27, 2003.
Steven Levy	"All Predators, All the Time? Maybe Not," *Newsweek*, July 3, 2006.
Walter Minkel	"Filters Block Needed Health Facts," *School Library Journal*, January 2003.
Geoffrey Nunberg	"Machines Make Moral Judgments, Selectively," *New York Times*, March 9, 2003.
Josh Politlove	"Bill Aims to Shield Kids from Online Porn," *Tampa (FL) Tribune*, March 7, 2006.
Sebastian Rupley	"Keep Your Kids Safe," *PC Magazine*, August 3, 2004.
John Schwartz	"The Pornography Industry vs. Digital Pirates," *New York Times*, February 8, 2004.
Barbara Dafoe Whitehead	"Online Porn," *Commonweal*, October 21, 2005.
Peter Wilkinson	"To Catch a Pedophile," *Rolling Stone*, March 4, 2004.

CHAPTER 4

Should Limits Be Placed on Online Pornography?

Chapter Preface

Online pornography is a relatively new form of media entertainment, and consequently, society is still struggling with how it should be classified. Some feel that Internet pornography should have its own set of rules and regulations, separate from those that govern other forms of pornography or other Internet subjects. These individuals usually believe that by singling out the medium and identifying what is and isn't pornographic, online pornography can be better contained and controlled. Others believe that online material should be subject to the same laws as print and movie pornography. In this debate, however, groups and individuals do not divide themselves neatly on liberal-conservative lines. They are mixed depending on the nuances of their beliefs.

Conservative pundit Jan LaRue, chief counsel for the conservative Concerned Women for America, argues strongly that pornography online should not be treated in a special manner—either more or less harshly than other forms. Differentiating Internet pornography could open the door to special treatment, she frequently writes. In a similar argument, the liberal Center for Democracy and Technology, whose motto is "working for civil liberties on the Internet," also urges that Internet pornography must not be singled out—either for government interference or protection. If parents want to protect their children, both argue, filters are the best way to do so. The Center for Democracy and Technology points to a National Academy of Science report that concluded "a combination of education, technology tools like filtering, and enforcement of existing laws was the appropriate way to protect kids online."

Others believe that making special laws and limits exclusively for online pornography is helpful. The Internet is a place like no other, some of these individuals argue, and should be given special treatment. Some groups that protect Internet rights, including pornography, subscribe to this point of view, such as Ynot.com, which bills itself as "the ultimate adult webmaster resource site." Interestingly, on most other issues The Center for Democracy and Technology and Ynot .com are in complete agreement. When it comes to special treatment for online pornography, however, they stand on opposite sides of the issue. This is just one example of the different viewpoints that will be illustrated in the following chapter.

> *"There are no convincing reasons why pornographic material should be limitless on the Internet while it is clearly limited elsewhere."*

Online Pornography Laws Should Be the Same as Other Pornography Laws

Pamela Paul

In the following viewpoint, author Pamela Paul argues that online pornography should be subject to the same laws and regulations that govern other forms of pornography, such as magazines and movies, as well as items like cigarettes, alcohol, or guns. American society does not have a problem restricting these potentially dangerous or damaging things—online pornography is no different. If those who wanted to view pornography online were required to enter a credit card number, minors could be easily restricted, and identities of predators traced. This would be similar to requiring someone to buy a ticket before an R-rated movie, Paul argues. Pamela Paul is an author and journalist who has written on marriage, family, and parenting. She published the 2002 book The Starter Marriage and the Future of Matrimony.

As you read, consider the following questions:

1. How did the Supreme Court define "obscenity" in the *Miller v. California* case, as cited by Paul?
2. What percentage of Americans believe pornography should be legal for all, according to the author?
3. What specific screening process does Paul recommend for online pornography?

Rather than fight for people's right to speak out against pornography, Americans have instead fought for the right of pornographers to distribute their product without regulation and for consumers to lap it up unhindered. "Isn't it our right to look at and read and masturbate to whatever we want?" has become a rallying cry. "What right does the government have in our bedrooms?" Businesses have made a fortune by linking pornography with civil liberties, arguing that to use pornography is to turn one's nose up at the Ed Meeses [author of a landmark pornography report] and the hypocritical reactionaries. They've managed to equate the use of pornography with a defense of the Bill of Rights, convincing an entire generation that pornography is not only okay, it's the American citizen's right. According to the *Pornified*/Harris poll, 23 percent of Americans believe that whether one likes it or not, people should have full access to pornography under the U.S. Constitution's First Amendment. Democrats were only slightly more likely (24 percent) than Republicans (20 percent) to take this position. Not surprisingly, those of the baby-boomer generation and younger are nearly twice as likely to believe pornography is protected speech than Americans age fifty-nine and older, and men are more than twice as likely as women to consider pornography a political right.

The major pornography lobbying group calls itself the Free Speech Coalition, much in the spirit of anti-environmentalist groups that adorn themselves in leafy labels like the Blue Skies Society to obscure their true agendas. The rhetoric of the pro-pornography movement also bears a striking resemblance to the gun rights movement. Each popularizes the idea of a Big Brother federal government tyranny out to strip Main Street citizens of their fundamental rights. Just as the Second Amendment was never intended to encourage the sale of semiautomatic military weapons to ex-cons, the First Amendment was never meant to sanction the dissemination of speech that is free of social merit, artistic quality, or political purpose. In a country obsessed with the Founding Fathers and their vision, little thought is given to what they would make of the current application of the Constitution's free political speech.

The Example of Larry Flynt

In the fight for freedom of porn, [*Hustler* magazine publisher] Larry Flynt—who once yelled [obscenities] at the Supreme Court . . . —positions himself as the Martin Luther King, Jr., of free speech, waging a battle for civil rights by endlessly contesting obscenity prosecutions on the basis of the First Amendment. He conveniently has the right set of enemies to rally his followers to the "liberal" cause. By going up against people like the Reverend Jerry Falwell of the Moral Majority, Flynt has turned himself into a martyr for supposed progressivism and "true" patriotism. The cover of Flynt's book *Sex, Lies, & Politics: The Naked Truth* features him posed in front of an oversized American flag. Meanwhile, his magazine *Hustler* has depicted violent and senseless forms of hardcore pornography, with one infamous spread depicting a woman shaved, raped, and apparently killed in a concentration camp–style setting. Those who refuse to play along with Flynt's constitutional ploy are ridiculed as reactionary and prudish. Yet even free speech advocates like *Harper's* [magazine] editor Lewis Lapham, who originally intended to lend his signature to a joint letter in support of Flynt against obscenity charges, withdrew his offer after viewing a copy of *Hustler*. "I'm not sure this was quite what [Thomas] Jefferson had in mind," he noted at the time. Flynt isn't the only businessman eager to equate his enterprise with constitutional freedom. The Playboy Foundation, for example, bestows an annual award loftily entitled the "Hugh M. Hefner First Amendment Award" to high school students, lawyers, journalists, and educators who protect Americans' right to free speech. Certainly people like [political pundits] Bill Maher and Molly Ivins, both recipients of the twenty-fifth anniversary award, deserve recognition for their efforts to promote free political speech, but the irony of an organization that disregards the rights of women giving such an honor is lost in the limelight of the celebrity-studded event. Those who defend pornographic images that denigrate women would be loath to defend [racist] *Little Black Sambo* books or Nazi artwork. But such hypocrisy and oversights are ignored on today's political battlefield over porn. Just what are we willing to tolerate in the name of "tolerance," and why?

Pornography vs. Sexual Expression

Rather than deal with the reality of pornographic material, there is a willful attempt on the part of pornographers and their defenders to portray pornography as something it clearly is not: a useful sexual education tool, a harmless form of recreation, open communication about sexuality. Lawyers for the ACLU [American Civil Liberties Union] frequently refer to "speech about sex" or "sexually oriented expression" instead of "pornography" when fighting measures intended to curb pornography. They argue that children will be prevented from accessing harmless and informative content about contraceptives and sexually transmitted diseases, that adults will be unable to read sexual material, such as sexually explicit essays or how-to

Defining Obscenity: A Supreme Court Decision

1. Obscene material is not protected by the First Amendment. A work may be subject to state regulation where that work, taken as a whole, appeals to the prurient interest in sex; portrays, in a patently offensive way, sexual conduct specifically defined by the applicable state law; and, taken as a whole, does not have serious literary, artistic, political, or scientific value.

Supreme Court of the United States,
Miller v. California, *June 21, 1973.*

guides on increasing sexual desire or skill. In the aftermath of the Child Online Protection Act's defeat by the Supreme Court [in 2004], Ann Beeson, the ACLU's associate legal director, said, "By preventing Attorney General [John] Ashcroft from enforcing this questionable federal law, the court has made it safe for artists, sex educators, and Web publishers to communicate with adults about sexuality without risking jail time." Perhaps sex educators, artists, and legitimate Web publishers *were* unfairly included in COPA's [Child Online Protection Act] targeted web, but many legal experts disagree with that analysis. And were that the case, the law could have been rewritten so as to confine its targets to pornography proper, allowing other sexually explicit forms of art and information to flourish. Instead, the law's opponents, including the ACLU, rushed to defend the right to free speech but neglected to differentiate between pornography and other forms of "sexual expression." As a result, what was once considered harmful, obscene, and dangerous is now exalted as free political speech. To call it "educational" or "speech about sex" smacks of legalistic semantics and intellectual dishonesty.

Harming Free Speech

By defending pornography as free speech, so-called advocates could actually be seen as threatening its foundations, as the Supreme Court noted in the 1973 *Miller v. California* obscenity case, the federal court's last major ruling defining pornography: "In our view, to equate the free and robust exchange of ideas and political debate with commercial exploitation of obscene material demeans the grand conception of the First Amendment and its high purposes in the historic struggle for freedom." According to the decision, obscenity—which is not protected by the Constitution's First Amendment—is material that a judge or jury finds is, as a whole, appealing to a prurient interest in sex, depicts sexual conduct in a patently offensive manner, and lacks serious literary, artistic, political, and scientific value. Using that definition, would [porn film] *Gag Factor 15* pass muster? How about the online how-to guide to creating an Asshole Milkshake? Until very recently, no one even conceived that the First Ammendment would apply to pornography, which was considered by common consent and by law to be unworthy of protection. Not only do pornographic images stretch the definition of "speech" but, as disseminated in the marketplace, they have a similar demonstrable effect on women as a white person making a threatening and vulgar racial epithet toward a black man or woman, which courts have already ruled to be unprotected by the First Amendment.

Moreover, rather than impose some kind of nationwide dictum, as its opponents suggest, the law in question gives considerable freedom to local communities to decide what's permissible. According to *Miller v. California*, localities are allowed to apply a "community standard" to make their own decisions about "obscenity" based on contemporary mores. A town can determine what kind of storefronts they want visible on Main Street or whether they want billboards advertising pornographic materials on their highways. Of course, the idea of "local community" shifted radically following the introduction of satellite television and the World Wide Web. A pornography shop operating on the wrong side of town can be easily opposed by a town council, but a Moscow-based Internet entrepreneur or even a San Fernando Valley pornography empire beaming their goods worldwide online does not easily fall under any local jurisdiction. But just because the community standard doesn't fit this new paradigm does not mean we should give up on it altogether.

Pornography Poll

A large majority of Americans aren't ready for defeatism either. According to a 2004 nationwide poll by Wirthlin Worldwide, 79 percent of Americans agree that laws against distributing obscene materials on the Internet should be vigorously enforced. (Democrats are as likely as Republicans to agree.) Despite the limitations of the community standard, a significant number of Americans (37 percent) believe pornography should be illegal to all and a majority (60 percent) believe it should be illegal to anyone under the age of eighteen. Surprisingly, men are significantly more likely than women to want pornography illegal for minors (69 percent of men versus 52 percent of women). Furthermore, *only 4 percent of Americans believe pornography should be legal for all.* If the local community doesn't exist on the World Wide Web, then perhaps we need a new standard, one that may not wipe out the world's pornography but could control its excesses within our nation's borders. In America today, it is easier to get pornography than it is to avoid it; we have protected the rights of those who wish to live in a pornified culture while altogether ignoring the interests of those who do not.

Some argue that what goes on in the privacy of an individual home isn't subject to any kind of community standard and therefore the Supreme Court's ruling doesn't apply. This argument, too, is shaky. Pornography affects not only the individual user but the user's family members, colleagues, and peers, as well as strangers and acquaintances with whom the user interacts every day. The effects of pornography extend well beyond the privacy of a single person's household. Moreover, what goes on inside a private home isn't a free-for-all. Husbands beat their wives inside the privacy of the home and kids are sexually molested and abused; though using pornography shouldn't be equated with such crimes, the common link is harm. Pornography need not be criminalized in order for it to be condemned.

Regulation for Other Media Forms

But once again we spend far less time criticizing pornography than we do in ensuring its existence and dissemination. People speak of Internet accessibility in hushed terms, as if an unfettered right to online material is the divine and essential right of man. Yet entertainment and information in all other media contain barriers to entry: Movies require the purchase of a ticket. Television is regulated in terms of what can appear: the language used on network sitcoms is restricted, and the programming a six-year-old is liable to encounter when he tunes in to cartoons on Saturday morning is clearly outlined by the federal government. Public libraries require people to apply for a library card, giving up "personal" information as a prerequisite for checking out material. Marketers are prevented from making unsolicited telemarketing phone calls to people who sign up for the Do Not Call registry, a regulation recently upheld by the Supreme Court.

Still, defenders of pornography argue that people have a constitutional right to access pornography on the Internet and requiring a screening process violates that right. "Screens drive away users," the ACLU has said. "Users don't want to give their credit card [numbers] in order to see material that is meant to be seen for free on the Web." But the "burden" of asking a person to use a credit card number in order to access materials is far from censorship. Rather, it is a small inconvenience, surmounted in a matter of seconds. If adults are rankled by the requirement, then they don't have to visit the pornography site, and can access pornography through other media—media that, incidentally, *are* restricted. Second, there's the false claim that such materials are "meant to be seen for free." Meant by whom? What omnipotent force deemed this the right of all citizens? True, pornographers offer free material to entice users into purchasing harder content. True, pornographic content may be pirated and offered for free to users, violating copyright law and ethical business practices, but that does not ensure that everyone necessarily must have the "right" to view pornography for free.

Limits Are Everywhere

More than a form of speech, pornography is a commercial product, manufactured and distributed by companies from one entrepreneur to huge corporations, and subject to the rules and ethics that govern commerce, not communication. Is oil censored? Are guns censored? Pharmaceuticals? Name a business in America that is not subject to trade regulations, taxes, zoning restrictions, pricing controls, distribution limitations. Asking an adult to punch in credit card numbers in order to access material is as much censorship as asking a youthful-looking adult trying to purchase cigarettes for proof that he or she is over eighteen. When people are carded at the movie theater for trying to enter an R-rated movie, nobody fights against it, championing their access to "free speech." The fact is, censorship already exists, if that's what one chooses to call it.

There are no convincing reasons why pornographic material should be limitless on the Internet while it is clearly limited elsewhere, but there are convincing arguments in favor of requiring credit card identification to gain access to pornography online. Perhaps punching in those numbers will offer consumers the opportunity to reconsider what they're doing rather than mindlessly looking at exploitative material. . . .

Such measures are tough to pass. Opponents of the courts' efforts to limit pornography raise pointed questions about just what would be included under "indecency" laws. What is "patently offensive," they ask, arguing that one person's standard might differ so radically from the next person's that it would lump committed homosexual coupling with hardcore images of women being brutalized. What lacks "serious" value? One person's estimation of offensive hardcore pornography might be the next person's erotica.

Pornography Does Not Equal Free Speech

Certainly, to get the government involved in people's private sex lives is a scary proposition. What's deemed dangerous by one person may be normal, even pleasurable to another. Reasonable people might assume that it's "obvious" what we mean by obscenity—a definition that would likely include violent pornography, scatological [related to excrement] porn, bukkake [ejaculating onto a person]—but it takes just one government administration to decree that all homosexual acts are obscene to understand why obscenity is an uneasy standard to enforce. Most Americans are probably like [Supreme Court] Justice Potter Stewart [who wrote the majority opinion in *Miller v. California*] when they say that while they cannot define pornography they know it when they see it. To pretend that the line between an R-rated film with depictions of sexuality and a XXX movie with hardcore double penetration and "money shots" is anywhere close to being blurred is willfully obtuse and plays into the worst fears of those who might otherwise naturally oppose pornography.

Nonetheless, we have to be able to draw a line somewhere; throwing up our hands, or defending the indefensible because the dilemma poses difficulty, is not the answer. The vast majority of Americans support the First Amendment, but pornography is not solely or even primarily an issue of free speech. Nor should one interpretation of the First Amendment be the only guideline, the only right, the only moral that matters. Just as pro-choice Americans can advocate fewer abortions while defending the right to have abortions, surely Americans can find practical ways to limit and regulate the pornified culture without challenging our constitutional foundations and rights. We shouldn't just worry about the consequences of banning pornography; we also need to worry about the consequences of letting porn proliferate unfettered. Pornography should move beyond a discussion of censorship and into one of standards.

> *"[The] court ... refused to consider the Internet any differently than it has ordinary mail. The court refuses to see the Internet as the unique community that it deserves to be recognized as."*

Online Pornography Laws Should Not Be the Same as Other Pornography Laws

Eric M. Winston

In the following viewpoint, attorney Eric M. Winston argues that "obscenity" on the Internet deserves a different definition—and set of laws—than apply to other media venues. Discussing a case in which a company was charged with distributing pornographic videos on the Internet as well as through the mail, Winston points out that the Internet has provided people with a far vaster array of ideas about what is "obscene" than ever before. New laws and regulations should be written to reflect this shift, he argues. Winston works on First Amendment, civil rights, and Internet industry legal issues.

As you read, consider the following questions:

1. What is the author's opinion of the "marketplace of ideas" theory?

2. What are two aspects of the definition of obscenity as written by the Supreme Court in *Miller v. California*, in Winston's opinion?

3. Why does the author argue that using "community standards" as applied to the Internet is obsolete?

On December 8, 2005 the United States Court of Appeals for the Third Circuit ruled that Extreme Associates, Inc. and its proprietors could be prosecuted . . . for the commercial distribution of obscene materials. The facts of the case are simple enough: Extreme Associates maintains a website through which it engages in the business of producing, selling and distributing obscene video tapes.

As a part of an undercover investigation, U.S Postal Inspectors purchased tapes by mail through the general public portion of the site. Inspectors also joined the members section of the website and downloaded and viewed video clips off of the site. Based upon this investigation, Extreme Associates was indicted in a ten charge count with, among other crimes, distributing obscene material through the mail and over the Internet.

Originally, the District Court, . . . dismissed the indictments against Extreme Associates because the statutes regulating the distribution of obscene material violated the constitution. In sum, the District Court ruled that the statutes regulating the distribution of obscenity were not narrowly tailored by the complete ban of distribution of obscene materials.

The Third Circuit did not analyze this matter on the basis of the First Amendment, but rather, through privacy grounds. . . . The court noted that the United States Supreme Court has consistently upheld the constitutionality of statutes

The Effect of Special Online Pornography Laws

When publishers have to stop and think about whether covering certain types of subjects could potentially land them in jail (or cause them to be blocked by censorware programs), you can bet that most will end up not running a potentially problematic story or linking to a potentially "objectionable" site. . . .

Overall, it's a bad deal for everyone.

Sean Carton, Publish, *April 21, 2006.*

regulating obscenity. In a bit of logic difficult for most to understand, the court has upheld the right to possess obscene material but not the right to distribute the material. In essence, one can own obscene material but have no legal way of obtaining it. In sum, the court found that there is no constitutional right to distribute obscene material and an individual could be prosecuted for distributing obscene material.

Internet a Unique Venue

This court (as have other courts) refused to consider the Internet any differently than it has ordinary mail. The court refuses to see the Internet as the unique community that it deserves to be recognized as. Although they rely on prior precedent to come to that conclusion, it does not take a Supreme Court Justice to see that the Internet has created a global community unlike any the world has seen. Never before have so many people had the ability to communicate in a way not even imagined only twenty years ago. With the ability to communicate comes the ability to share ideas and thoughts. [Former Supreme Court] Justice Oliver Wendell Holmes brilliantly espoused the theory of the "marketplace of ideas." This theory should be the cornerstone for all free expression in this country. It is the theory that all ideas should be freely expressed and explored so that a person can make the best decision possible.

The Internet gives us the ultimate marketplace of ideas. In the past, only the most powerful and wealthy could truly give their opinion to the public through newspaper, radio and television. Today, the Internet allows virtually anyone with access to a computer the ability to reach a worldwide audience. Individuals' webpages and blogs give all of us the chance to voice an opinion to the masses for a relatively small amount of money. It is time that the Internet was treated differently than other forms of media because of its unique nature. The Internet itself transforms our concepts of sexually explicit and obscene material. It gives us the ability to experience life through the eyes of many different people with many different outlooks. Our concepts of obscenity are altered by the Internet's ability to present us with a vast array of ideas and concepts that people may never have considered before. Since the Internet knows no boundaries, neither do the authorities who prosecute obscenity-based crimes. It is time that a standard of obscenity was created that encompasses the vastness of the Internet.

Take note for the purposes of the motion in the Third Circuit decision of *Extreme Associates*. Extreme Associates stipulated that the material available on its website was legally obscene. In order to be prosecuted under the statute for distributing material that is obscene, the material actually must be obscene. This decision by the Court did not even address the issue of obscenity but merely brushed it under the rug. Ironically, what is legally obscene is still a source of great debate. The United States Supreme Court in [*Miller v. California* in] 1973 concocted a convoluted test wherein obscenity was measured by:

1. Whether "the average person, applying contemporary community standards" would find that the work, taken as a whole, appeals to the prurient interest,

2. Whether the work depicts or describes, in a patently offensive way, sexual conduct specifically defined by the applicable state law, and

3. Whether the work, taken as a whole, lacks serious literary, artistic, political, or scientific value.

A Definition of Obscenity

This "test" (for lack of a better word) for identifying obscene materials has confused scholars and mystics alike. It creates a patchwork formula in which one must consider local community standards and whether the work has any redeeming social value under national standards. Furthermore, the test asks us to evaluate whether the work would appeal to prurient interests (prurient interests defined as: a morbid, degrading and unhealthy interest in sex, as distinguished from a mere candid interest in sex). Therefore, courts have to consider what the difference is between a morbid interest in sex and a candid interest in sex. In reality, there are no clear guidelines for what is and is not obscene. One man's fetish is another man's delight. Truly, beauty is in the eye of the beholder and the courts have not found a way to distinguish in a meaningful way how to define what is obscene. Reliance on shifting community standards creates a chameleon like definition which changes depending on where you live. Unfortunately, the most apt description of obscenity comes from [Supreme Court] Justice Potter Stewart when he candidly states:

> "Criminal laws in this area are constitutionally limited to hard-core pornography. I shall not today attempt further to define the kinds of material I understand to be embraced within that shorthand description; and perhaps I could never succeed in intelligibly doing so. But I know it when I see it. . . ."

The Supreme Court should provide the public with a bright line definition of obscenity. Possibly, the *United States of America v. Extreme Associates* decision by the Third Circuit will give the Supreme Court a chance to rework the definition of obscenity to something more measured and ascertainable. They ask us to rely on community standards when the Internet itself defies the concept of local community. This decision highlights the failure of the "community standards" definition as applied to the Internet. As stated above, it is time that the courts come up to date with the times. With our ability to see and hear virtually anything we can imagine, a thirty year old concept of obscenity has no relevance for today. Technology has made many of the old concepts of obscenity obsolete. Since the Internet stretches across the globe it is impossible to identify a community standard that would be relevant to every community that the Internet reaches. Just because technology has outpaced the court it does not mean that people should be prosecuted for that reason. In *United States of America v. Extreme Associates,* the Third Circuit ignores the unique nature of the Internet. It is time that obscenity is defined in such a manner as to meet contemporary standards and recognize the impact that the Internet has had on our society. It is clear that when anaylzing Internet cases, community standards should not be relevant, rather an Internet standard should be created for the global community that it serves.

> "[The] .xxx debate has revealed just how difficult it could be to create an alternative form of [Internet] governance . . . . For the moment . . . ICANN seems like the best bet."

A Pornography Web Domain Should Be Created

Celeste Biever

In 2000, an Internet registry company asked the Internet Corporation for Assigned Names and Numbers (ICANN), the agency that authorizes Internet domains, to create a special "dot" Web domain specifically for pornographic materials: .xxx. In the following viewpoint, Celeste Biever argues that while there certainly are problems with pornography on the Internet, establishing the new domain is not one of them. Politicians, governmental agencies, and nonprofit organizations have used the proposal to further their own agendas, she writes, rather than addressing the real issue: how to properly govern the Internet. Celeste Biever is a reporter for the British magazine New Scientist.

As you read, consider the following questions:

1. What major organization came out against the proposed Web domain, according to the author?

2. What was the Family Research Council's response to the .xxx Web domain, according to Biever?

3. What is one aspect the debate over .xxx has revealed, according to the author?

Editor's Note: On May 10, 2006, ICANN voted against establishing a .xxx Web domain. In March 2006, U.S. senators Max Baucus and Mark Pryor introduced the Cyber Safety for Kids Act, which requires the federal government to work with ICANN to create a special domain for pornographic material. The bill was still in committee as of the time of the present volume's publication.

When the internet company ICM Registry proposed the creation of a virtual red light district in 2000, fenced in by a .xxx web address suffix or "top level domain" (TLD), it was hoping to create revenue by providing a new business opening for pornographers.

The company, based in Jupiter, Florida, plans to make money leasing out domain names such as www.toys.xxx at a rate of $60 a year, in return for operating the databases that connect internet users to the servers hosting porn. The idea is that the .xxx domain will make it easier for users and search engines to identify porn sites. ICM claims this will help clean up cyberspace by providing a straightforward way to keep pornography separate from the rest of the web.

Initially, others seemed to agree. On 1 June [2005], the proposal won approval from the Internet Corporation for Assigned Names and Numbers (ICANN), a powerful US-based non-profit organisation that decides which TLDs will be used. The move was also backed by several US politicians, on the

The Need for a Pornography Web Domain

"While the Internet is an exceptional learning tool, it allows children the same easy access to websites about space shuttles as it does for pornography. Turning a blind eye to this problem has allowed the online pornography industry to expand and enabled kids to view adult content at very young ages," Pryor said. "By corralling pornography in its own domain, our bill provides parents with the ability to create a 'do not enter zone' for their kids."

Office of Mark Pryor, March 16, 2006. www.senate.gov/˜pryor.

grounds that it will make it easier for filtering software to protect children and others who do not wish to be exposed to porn.

Divided Political Opinion

ICANN might reasonably have expected its proposal to face some opposition too, but no one predicted the hornet's nest of political activity that has ensued. The American Civil Liberties Union (ACLU), for example, came out against it. "It's dangerous from a free speech aspect," says Mary Johnson of ACLU. "How do you define what content is porn and what is just a Victoria's Secret ad?" Politicians, civil liberties groups, conservative organisations, members of the [George W.] Bush administration and other governments have all joined the debate.

But some are exploiting the dispute to push agendas that have little to do with pornography. Behind the commotion over .xxx is a larger battle over control of the Internet itself. "The current dispute is sort of bogus," says Esther Dyson, former chair of ICANN. "It's political football." And when the

US Department of Commerce, together with ICANN's Governmental Advisory Committee (GAC), which comprises over 100 representatives of governments around the world, persuaded ICANN to postpone final approval of the .xxx domain, many observers started to suspect that something underhanded was going on.

The Department of Commerce, among others, hopes this delay will allow ICANN to reverse its decision. The ultraconservative, non-profit Family Research Council based in Washington DC says .xxx lends porn an undeserved legitimacy, and gives pornographers "even more opportunities to flood our homes, libraries, and society with pornography."

Opposition to the .xxx domain has also been voiced by several foreign governments. At a recent meeting of the GAC in Luxembourg, the possibility of .xxx was hotly debated. Brazil and Denmark were the most outspoken in opposition to .xxx. But while these countries claim they are motivated by a dislike of pornography, observers are finding this difficult to take at face value. "Let's just say that neither of those two countries is prudish," says Milton Mueller of Syracuse University in New York, who founded the Internet Governance Project, a consortium of academics researching the internet, and was a sceptical observer at the meeting. "It's all about a political opportunity to go after ICANN."

ICANN Best Choice

The dispute is a headache ICANN can do without, as it tries to tread a fine line between critics from abroad, who say it is too strongly influenced by the US government, and those in the government itself who want to rein it in. The Department of Commerce controls the Internet's master look-up table, so it could overrule any decision ICANN made on the .xxx issue if it wanted to. But till now, it has never exploited its power to do this, and has always endorsed ICANN's decisions.

If ICANN does fall into line with the Department of Commerce this time, and fails to approve the .xxx domain name, its decision will be seized on by those countries trying to wrest governance of the Internet from the US. Their main forum is the World Summit on the Information Society (WSIS) organised by the International Telecommunications Union. . . . "The major external check on ICANN is its fear that its powers will be seized away by the WSIS meetings," says Michael Froomkin of the University of Miami Law School in Florida, who is editor of the website Icannwatch.com. If, however, ICANN sticks to its guns, the US government could decide to curtail its independence.

To make matters worse for ICANN, the debate has exposed many of its weaknesses, such as its failure to hold open meetings, to stick to procedures for making decisions, and its propensity for ad hoc rulings. It badly needs to evolve to answer its critics.

But ICANN may yet win the day. Its trump card is that the .xxx debate has revealed just how difficult it could be to create an alternative form of governance. Most independent observers agree that however the Internet is governed, it should remain free and open. For the moment, to maintain this freedom, ICANN seems like the best bet.

A Pornography Web Domain Should Not Be Created

Declan McCullagh

In this viewpoint, Declan McCullagh argues that establishing a .xxx Web domain specifically for pornography would allow governments to restrict the free speech of legal pornographic and nonpornographic sites. Taking a .xxx Web address is supposed to be voluntary at first, McCullagh writes, but before long, legitimate educational or informational sites that contain sexual material could be forced to adopt the domain name. This would be a form of censorship, the author argues. Declan McCullagh is a writer and photographer who works out of San Francisco.

As you read, consider the following questions:

1. For how much was entrepreneur Stuart Lawley proposing to sell the .xxx domain names, according to McCullagh?

2. What problem does the author predict for sites such as Salon.com or Playboy.com if .xxx is launched?

3. What is the ACLU's real concern with the .xxx proposal, according to McCullagh?

Stuart Lawley, a 41-year-old entrepreneur in Jupiter, Fla., is the unlikely champion for the online equivalent of a red-light district. A British citizen, Lawley swears that he's no smut seller himself. "I have no current or historic links to the adult industry in any form," he asserts.

That appears to be true. Lawley started Oneview.net, a U.K. business Internet provider, in the 1990s and cashed out at the height of the dot-com craze in March 2000. A profile in the [Manchester, U.K.] *Guardian* newspaper a few months earlier pegged his net worth to be in the tens of millions of dollars.

After a brief, sunny retirement in the Bahamas, where he learned how to golf and spear fish, Lawley moved to Florida and got the itch to get involved with the Internet again.

"Sex is a very big area on the Internet," Lawley said. "Our research staff surprised me. I couldn't believe how prevalent it was and what the actual statistics were for the number of sites and the number of users."

Under his proposal, submitted to the Internet Corporation for Assigned Names and Numbers (ICANN), .xxx domain names would be sold for $70 to $75 each. Child pornography would be verboten, but pretty much anything else would be permissible, Lawley said. "Apart from child pornography, which is completely illegal, we're really not in the content-monitoring business."

Instead, Lawley and his partners are in the business to make money. A report from Reuters Business Insights in February 2003 calculated that sex represented two-thirds of all online content revenue in 2001 and that it had ballooned to a $2.5 billion industry since then. Lawley estimates that 25 per-

Parents Are the Best Solution

Parents must do their job. Filtering—not just filtering software but filtered online services apart from the broader Internet that might be appropriate for the very young—is available. . . .

Another tool at parents' disposal is tracking software that lets them monitor everything a child does or has done on the Internet—filtered or not.

Spying? Maybe. But it's up to the family. And it is less restrictive than regulating content on the entire Internet.

Clyde Wayne Crews Jr., San Diego Union-Tribune, *May 17, 2002.*

cent of all Internet search queries are related to sex and that more than a million adult domain names exist. Owning the rights to sell pieces of .xxx real estate, he concluded, would be a perfect way to make money off consumers' insatiable appetite for online raunch and ribaldry.

Free-Expression Issues

The way the proposed .xxx registry would work is twofold. Lawley's company, ICM Registry, would handle the technical aspects of running the master database of .xxx sex sites. For its troubles, it would charge $60 a domain name and let resellers add their own markup of perhaps $10 to $15 per domain.

A second, nonprofit organization, the International Foundation for Online Responsibility would be in charge of setting the rules for .xxx. It would have a seven-person board of directors, including a child advocacy advocate, a free-expression aficionado and, naturally, at least one person from the adult entertainment industry. As president and chairman of ICM Registry, Lawley gives himself just one vote on the board.

The foundation's charter is intentionally quite protective of free speech. It aims to "protect the privacy and security of consenting adult consumers of online adult entertainment goods and services" and references the free-expression principles in the United Nations Universal Declaration of Human Rights.

Unlike other online suggestions for innocuous top-level domains like .travel or .jobs, the proposal for .xxx plunges the Internet into a U.S. political stew that's already at a roiling boil. The Federal Communications Commission has recently been tossing around penalties for "indecent" radio broadcasts, while [former] Attorney General John Ashcroft has indicated that a crackdown on obscene Web sites is about to take place.

The problem, in other words, is that as soon as .xxx launches, conservatives in Congress will begin to clamor for laws to make the domain mandatory for sex-related Web sites. That may not be a big deal for hard-core pornmeisters who prefer that virtual street address, but what about sex education sites that include explicit graphics and don't wish to be blocked by filtering software? And where should Salon.com—which features images of topless women—or Playboy.com—which publishes important interviews with U.S. presidents—end up?

Protecting Children

This is not just a theoretical concern. Back in 2000, before Lawley got involved as president, ICM Registry applied to run the .xxx domain. But ICANN shot down the proposal.

It didn't take Congress long to get involved. At a hearing in February 2001, Rep. Fred Upton, R-Mich., demanded to know why ICANN didn't approve .xxx "as a means of protecting our kids from the awful, awful filth which is sometimes widespread on the Internet." Sen. Joseph Lieberman, D-Conn., griped to a federal commission that .xxx was necessary to force adult Webmasters to "abide by the same standard as the proprietor of an X-rated movie theater."

To his credit, Lawley is pledging a legal defense fund of $250,000 to "maintain the voluntary nature of the domain name system." He's also hired Robert Corn-Revere, a top-notch lawyer . . . , who has represented Playboy Entertainment Group before the U.S. Supreme Court, to research whether Congress could get away with ordering sex-themed Web sites to slap .xxx at the end of their address. Corn-Revere's conclusion: The .xxx folks "should prevail in any ensuing litigation, if any attempt is made by the government to require registration in a .xxx domain."

Barry Steinhardt, head of the ACLU's technology and liberty program, isn't nearly as optimistic. "I am not quite so confident that we will prevail" under existing First Amendment precedents, Steinhardt said.

But the ACLU's real concerns with the proposal lie overseas. "There are nations all over the world that will undoubtedly try to force Web sites into the .xxx (top-level domain) or to block Web sites in it that they somehow view as offensive," Steinhardt said. "I don't think the operators have taken sufficient account of that problem. It will become a worldwide red-light district for the Internet, into which speakers who have free-expression rights and should be able to reach a mass audience will be forced."

Maybe U.S. politicians have matured [since 2001]. Perhaps courts can now be trusted to do the right thing, upholding the First Amendment's guarantee of freedom of expression. But given that the House of Representatives voted by an 18-to-1 margin [in August 2005] to boost the penalties for "profane" broadcasts, the initially voluntary .xxx district may turn out to be a one-way street.

Periodical Bibliography

The following articles have been selected to supplement the diverse view presented in this chapter.

Center for Democracy and Technology	Letter to Max Baucus, March 23, 2006. www.cdt.org.
Eve Fairbanks	"The Porn Identity," *New Republic*, February 6, 2006.
John Foley	"Can't Ignore Technology and the Fight Against Child Porn," *InformationWeek*, February 14, 2005. www.informationweek.com.
Brian Friel	"The War on Kiddie Porn," *National Journal*, March 25, 2006.
Rebecca Gray	"www.xxx.not," *Print*, July/August 2004.
Burt Helm	"A Hot Domain on Ice," *BusinessWeek Online*, April 7, 2006. www.businessweek.com.
David Ho	"Risqué Web Sites to Be '.XXX'-Rated," *Atlanta Journal-Constitution*, June 3, 2005.
Wendy Koch	"In the Shadows of the Net, War on Child Porn Rages," *USA Today*, October 17, 2006.
Jan LaRue	"Lame-Brain Porn Domain," *Concerned Women for America*, March 21, 2006, www.cwfa.org.
Seth Lubove	"Sex Sells," *Forbes*, June 6, 2005.
Robert S. Mueller III	"Child Pornography and the Internet," *Vital Speeches of the Day*, January 1, 2007.
John Naughton	"Let's Put Internet Porn on a New Top Shelf," *Observer* (London), September 4, 2005.
Christopher Rhoads	"Plan for Adult Area Sparks a Fight on Control of Web," *Wall Street Journal*, May 10, 2006.

For Further Discussion

Chapter 1

1. In Viewpoint 4, J.D. Obenberger argues that online pornography cannot be classified as immoral since a majority of the population makes use of it. Do you agree or disagree with this line of reasoning? Does gauging morality hinge on the views of the majority? Does an immoral act become moral if enough people engage in it? Explain your answer.

2. In Viewpoint 5, Rod Gustafson argues that online pornography can be addictive and dangerous. He acknowledges, though, that he is referring to its effects on the individual. Can something that affects the individual be harmful to society as a whole? Why or why not?

Chapter 2

1. The Supreme Court ruled in 2004 that the Child Online Protection Act (COPA) was not constitutional. Nonetheless, many believed the act should have remained in place. After carefully reading the opinion of Anthony Kennedy and the opposing viewpoint by Judith Reisman, state whether you agree or disagree with the Court's decision and explain your reasoning.

2. Groups opposing regulation of online pornography frequently use the term "censorship," as in Michael J. Miller's article. Groups favoring regulation avoid this term, referring instead to "protection," as in Robert Peters' argument. Does the use of specific words enhance or detract from the author's credibility, in your opinion? Why?

Chapter 3

1. Paul J. Cambria Jr. is an attorney for the adult entertainment industry. In his testimony before Congress, he argues that no further regulation is needed to protect children from online pornography. He cites reliable statistics and facts, yet he is paid to defend pornography. Does this self-interest affect how you view his argument? Why or why not?

2. Don S. Otis brings up the issue of children's rights in his viewpoint. In his opinion, whatever rights children do have do not trump their need for protection. Do you agree or disagree with this line of reasoning? Do children have rights at all, and if they do, should those rights be upheld by law? What differences are there, in your opinion, between the rights of children and those of adults?

3. After reading all of the viewpoints in this chapter, whom do you think is responsible for protecting children from online pornography: the government or parents? Use evidence from the viewpoints to support your answer.

Chapter 4

1. Pamela Paul argues that Americans have placed restrictions on plenty of harmful materials. She uses the specific examples of cigarettes, alcohol, and guns to make her point. Consider these items. How are they the same or different from pornography in their intent and potential to harm? In your opinion, were these good comparisons to make? Why or why not?

2. In many of the viewpoints in this chapter, and in the book, authors point out that the Internet in America is virtually unregulated, unlike most other forms of media. Do you think this quality should be preserved? What are the advantages and disadvantages to general regulation of the Internet, including that of pornographic material? Explain your reasoning.

Organizations to Contact

The editors have compiled the following list of organizations concerned with the issues debated in this book. The descriptions are derived from materials provided by the organizations. All have publications or information available for interested readers. The list was compiled on the date of publication of the present volume; the information provided here may change. Be aware that many organizations take several weeks or longer to respond to inquiries, so allow as much time as possible.

Adult Freedom Foundation (AFF)
119 E. Montgomery Ave., Suite 2, Ardmore, PA   19003
(610) 896-5558
Web site: www.adultfreedomfoundation.org

The Adult Freedom Foundation is a watchdog group for the adult entertainment industry and works to protect that industry's First Amendment rights. The foundation provides legal counsel and litigation, as well as media and government access to adult entertainment experts. The AFF maintains an archive of news relating to adult entertainment on its Web site.

American Civil Liberties Union (ACLU)
132 W. Forty-third St., New York, NY   10036
(212) 944-9800 • fax: (212) 359-5290
Web site: www.aclu.org

The ACLU is the nation's oldest and largest civil liberties organization. The ACLU provides legal defense, research and education and publishes the monthly newsletter *Civil Liberties Alert*, as well as pamphlets, books, and position papers on pornography and other issues.

Concerned Women for America (CWA)
1015 Fifteenth St. NW, Suite 1100, Washington, DC   20005
(202) 488-7000 • fax: (202) 488-0806
Web site: www.cwfa.org

CWA's purpose is to preserve, protect, and promote traditional Judeo-Christian values through education, legislative action, and other activities. It is concerned with creating an environment that is conducive to building strong families and raising healthy children. CWA opposes pornography in the media and publishes the monthly *Family Voice*, which periodically addresses the issue.

Ethics and Public Policy Center (EPPC)
1015 Fifteenth St. NW, Suite 900, Washington, DC   20005
(202) 682-1200 • fax: (202) 408-0632
e-mail: ethics@eppc.org
Web site: www.eppc.org

The Ethics and Public Policy Center is a think tank that works to apply the Judeo-Christian moral tradition to issues of public policy, including censorship and pornography. The EPPC provides experts and scholars to media sources and provides research resources for scholars. The center publishes numerous books and articles by its members.

Family Research Council (FRC)
801 G St. NW, Washington, DC   20001
(202) 393-2100 • fax: (202) 393-2134
Web site: www.frc.org

The council seeks to promote and protect the interests of the traditional family. It focuses on issues such as parental autonomy and responsibility, community support for single parents, and protecting children from inappropriate images in the media. The FRC publishes policy papers, position statements, and books such as *The ACLU vs. America: Exposing the Agenda to Redefine Moral Values*.

First Amendment Center

1101 Wilson Blvd., Arlington, VA   22209
(703) 528-0800 • fax: (703) 284-2879
e-mail: info@fac.org
Web site: www.firstamendmentcenter.org

The First Amendment Center works to protect First Amendment rights through information and education, including freedom of speech and freedom of information. The center provides extensive research resources at its Virginia and Nashville, Tennessee, offices as well as online. The center publishes a yearly report, *The State of the First Amendment*, as well as guest editorials, pamphlets, and educational materials.

Focus on the Family

8605 Explorer Dr., Colorado Springs, CO   80920
(719) 531-3400 • fax: (719) 531-3424
Web site: www.family.org

Focus on the Family is a Christian organization dedicated to preserving and strengthening the traditional family. Focus on the Family opposes the presence of pornography on the Internet and supports government controls and parental supervision to combat it. Focus on the Family publishes numerous articles on its Web site, such as "Helping Your Child Navigate the Blogosphere."

Free Speech Coalition

PO Box 10480, Canoga Park, CA   91309
(818) 348-9373 • fax: 818-886-5914
Web site: www.freespeechcoalition.org

The Free Speech Coalition is the trade association for the adult entertainment industry. The group lobbies Congress on behalf of adult entertainment providers, provides public education, and functions as a legislative watchdog for the industry. The coalition publishes a weekly update, the *Free Speech X-Press,* as well as a biannual magazine, *Free Speaker.*

Morality in Media (MIM)
475 Riverside Dr., Suite 239, New York, NY   10115
(212) 870-3222 • fax: (212)-870-2765
e-mail: mim@moralityinmedia.org
Web site: www.moralityinmedia.org

Morality in Media is a nonprofit organization that works to combat obscenity and uphold decency standards in the media. The group works to fight online pornography by providing information on its Web site, as well as maintaining the National Obscenity Law Center, a clearinghouse of legal materials on obscenity law. MIM publishes the *Morality in Media Newsletter* as well as two online monthly columns for parents.

Protect Every Child
PO Box 749, Knightdale, NC   27545
e-mail: soapbox@protecteverychild.org
Web site: www.protecteverychild.org

Protect Every Child is a nonprofit organization that works to educate parents and children about Internet safety. The organization is opposed to the presence of unregulated pornography online. Protect Every Child publishes an occasional newsletter on its Web site, as well as providing a forum for testimonials from pornography opponents.

Bibliography of Books

Carlos A. Arnaldo *Child Abuse on the Internet: Ending the Silence.* New York: Berghahn, 2001.

Lyndon Bowring *Searching for Intimacy: Pornography, the Internet and the XXX Factor.* Fort Worth, TX: Authentic, 2005.

Patrick Carnes *In the Shadows of the Net: Breaking Free of Compulsive Online Sexual Behavior.* Center City, MN: Hazelden, 2004.

D. Kirk Davidson *Selling Sin: The Marketing of Socially Unacceptable Products.* Westport, CT: Praeger, 2003.

Murray Dry *Civil Peace and the Quest for Truth: The First Amendment Freedoms in Political Philosophy and American Constitutionalism.* Lanham, MD: Lexington, 2004.

Monique Mattei Ferraro *Investigating Child Exploitation and Pornography: The Internet, the Law, and Forensic Science.* Burlington, MA: Elsevier Academic, 2005.

Bruce E. Fleming *Sexual Ethics: Liberal vs. Conservative.* Lanham, MD: University Press of America, 2004.

John H. Gagnon *Sexual Conduct: The Social Sources of Human Sexuality.* New Brunswick, NJ: Aldine Transaction, 2005.

Craig Gross | *The Dirty Little Secret: Uncovering the Truth Behind Porn.* Grand Rapids, MI: Zondervan, 2006.

Mathias Kland and Andrew Murray, eds. | *Human Rights in the Digital Age.* London: Glass House, 2005.

Marty Klein | *America's War on Sex: The Attack on Law, Lust, and Liberty.* Westport, CT: Praeger, 2006.

Frederick Lane | *Obscene Profits: Entrepreneurs of Pornography in the Cyber Age.* Oxford, UK: Routledge, 2001.

Peter Lehman | *Pornography: Film and Culture.* New Brunswick, NJ: Rutgers University Press, 2006.

Marlene M. Maheu | *Infidelity on the Internet: Virtual Relationships and Real Betrayal.* Naperville, IL: Sourcebooks, 2001.

Joan Mason-Grant | *Pornography Embodied: From Speech to Sexual Practice.* Lanham, MD: Rowman & Littlefield, 2004.

Michael A. McBain | *Internet Pornography: Awareness and Prevention.* Lincoln, NE: Writers' Club Press, 2002.

National Research Council | *Youth, Pornography and the Internet.* Washington, DC: National Academies Press, 2002.

Ethel Quayle | *Child Pornography.* Oxford, UK: Routledge, 2003.

Ethel Quayle and Max Taylor, eds.
Viewing Child Pornography on the Internet: Understanding the Offence, Managing the Offender, Helping the Victims. Lyme Regis, UK: Russell House, 2005.

Gil Reavill
Smut: A Sex Industry Insider (and Concerned Father) Says Enough Is Enough. New York: Sentinel, 2005.

Phyllis Schlafly
The Supremacists: The Tyranny of Judges and How to Stop It. Dallas, TX: Spence, 2006.

Kevin B. Skinner
Treating Pornography Addiction: The Essential Tool for Recovery. Provo, UT: GrowthClimate, 2005.

L.W. Sumner
The Hateful and the Obscene: Studies in the Limits of Free Expression. Buffalo, NY: University of Toronto Press, 2004.

Raymond Tatalovich and Byron W. Daynes, eds.
Moral Controversies in American Politics. Armonk, NY: M.E. Sharpe, 2005.

Maxwell Taylor
Child Pornography: An Internet Crime. New York: Brunner-Routledge, 2003.

Amy White
Virtually Obscene: The Case for an Uncensored Internet. Jefferson, NC: McFarland, 2006.

Index